HEARTSTRINGS

H E A R T S T R I N G S

MARJORIE LIN KYRIOPOULOS

Epigraph Books
Rhinebeck, New York

Paperback ISBN 978-1-954744-15-8
eBook ISBN 978-1-954744-16-5

Library of Congress Control Number 2021907164

Cover painting by Kris Lange, krislangeart.com
Book design by Colin Rolfe

Epigraph Books
22 East Market Street, Suite 304
Rhinebeck, NY 12572
(845) 876-4861
epigraphps.com

HeartStrings is dedicated to my Aunt Wanda,
my grandmother Katina,
my mother, Afton,
my children, Bill and Liz,
and my grandchildren, James, Hawa Marie, and Sophie Anne
with deep love and gratitude.

ACKNOWLEDGMENTS

~

I AM ETERNALLY GRATEFUL FOR:

My grandparents, Katina and William, whose deep love for each other is my legacy.

My beautiful Aunt Wanda, who inspired me to take this journey.

My parents, who were always there for me when I needed them most.

All my aunts and uncles who held me in their arms, virtually, as I wrote these stories.

My brother Frank and my sisters Kathy, Mary, Debbie, Jami, and (sis-in-law) Christine for putting up with my smarty pants attitude.

My first best friend, Susan Christensen.

All my early readers, especially Carmen, Marcus, Michelle, Athina, Mindy, Lyn, Jami, and Peg.

My friend and final editor, Elaine.

My coach, Mary Carroll Moore, for her help and support during the messy writing process.

My publisher, Epigraph Publishing, especially Colin Rolfe, who guided me through the self-publishing process.

My friend and former colleague, Kris Lange, who created "Flowers on Turquoise" (cover art) just in time for me to serendipitously discover it.

Everyone everywhere who has made a difference in my life.

I am also grateful for these generous permissions to reprint excerpts from previously published work:

innerbody.com, "Chordae Tendineae," October 27, 2017

Helen (Zeese) Papanikolas, "The Greeks in Utah," Utah History Encyclopedia

American Heart Association, Inc., "Is Broken Heart Syndrome Real?"

Dan Hurley, "Grandma's Experiences Leave a Mark on Your Genes," Discover Magazine, June 25, 2015

Maurice Bassett, *Reverence for Life: The Words of Albert Schweitzer*, from a letter written shortly before his death, 1965

David Bottoms, "In a U-Haul North of Damascus"

Will Kuan, "Japan's Colorful Gravestone Decorations Protect the Souls of Lost Children," atlasobscura.com/articles/jizo-cemetery-statues, April 6, 2017

Terry Tempest Williams, *When Women were Birds: Fifty-Four Variations on Voice*, Picador, February 2013

CONTENTS

~

Chordae Tendineae — xiii

Introduction — xv

Foreword — xix

Three Generations — xxi

   My Mother's Generation — xxii

   My Generation — xxiii

   My Children's Generation — xxiv

Prologue — xxv

PART 1. THE GREEK AMERICAN DREAM

My Grandparents — 3

I Can't Give You Anything But Love — 5

Life and Death in Pocatello — 11

Katina Knows Things — 15

The Early Years — 21

Banished to Sacramento — 29

PART 2. MY MOTHER'S GENERATION

The Chaus Sisters   37
Secrets and Lies in Salt Lake City   39
Happiness   44
Some Enchanted Evening   50
Fools Rush In   53
The Chaus Brothers   60
Work Work Work   62
Friend or Foe?   64
Love and Marriage   68
The Deer Hunting Mishap   71

PART 3. STAGES OF GRIEF

And Then There Were Three   81
Memory Eternal   83
Love is Blind   86
The Unimaginable   90
In Memoriam   94
Beware of Greeks Bearing Gifts   97
Life is Good   101
The Case of the Missing Stamp Collection   106
The Rest of the Story   109

PART 4. MY GENERATION

My Guardian Angel   119
Santa Claus and Elvis Presley   122
On the Road Again   127
"It Wasn't an Accident"   129
Reverence for Life   132

CONTENTS

~

Chordae Tendineae   xiii

Introduction   xv

Foreword   xix

Three Generations   xxi

    My Mother's Generation   xxii

    My Generation   xxiii

    My Children's Generation   xxiv

Prologue   xxv

PART 1. THE GREEK AMERICAN DREAM

My Grandparents   3

I Can't Give You Anything But Love   5

Life and Death in Pocatello   11

Katina Knows Things   15

The Early Years   21

Banished to Sacramento   29

PART 2. MY MOTHER'S GENERATION

The Chaus Sisters	37
Secrets and Lies in Salt Lake City	39
Happiness	44
Some Enchanted Evening	50
Fools Rush In	53
The Chaus Brothers	60
Work Work Work	62
Friend or Foe?	64
Love and Marriage	68
The Deer Hunting Mishap	71

PART 3. STAGES OF GRIEF

And Then There Were Three	81
Memory Eternal	83
Love is Blind	86
The Unimaginable	90
In Memoriam	94
Beware of Greeks Bearing Gifts	97
Life is Good	101
The Case of the Missing Stamp Collection	106
The Rest of the Story	109

PART 4. MY GENERATION

My Guardian Angel	119
Santa Claus and Elvis Presley	122
On the Road Again	127
"It Wasn't an Accident"	129
Reverence for Life	132

Sunday Mornings	136
Let it Be	137
Que Será, Será	144
The Road Less Traveled	149
The Beginning of the End	162
Crazy	171
Pilgrim	193
Suicide is Painless	203
The Sins of the Father	213
Tender Mercies	220
It Runs in the Family	224

PART 5. FUTURE GENERATIONS

Forgiveness	231
Epilogue	235

CHORDAE TENDINEAE

~

"The chordae tendineae are a group of tough, tendinous strands in the heart. They are commonly referred to as the 'heart strings' since they resemble small pieces of string. Functionally, the chordae tendineae play a vital role in holding the atrioventricular valves in place while the heart is pumping blood."

—WWW.INNERBODY.COM

~

HEARTSTRINGS IS A memoir about an outwardly loving, Greek-American family whose matriarch (my maternal grandmother) fled the island of Crete in 1915 to join her brothers, George and John Liviakis, in Pocatello, Idaho. A year later, my grandmother, Katina, met my grandfather, Vasili.

Grandpa's Greek name was Vassilios Demetriou Tsausis. At some point, my grandfather changed his name to William Demitrius Chaus. Although his last name was sometimes spelled with an "e" on the end, Chause, eventually he settled on Chaus. My mother's family wanted to be American but they weren't sure how to spell the American version of Tsaousis.

After my grandparents were married, they moved to Utah where they raised six children on a small farm southeast of Salt Lake City near 38th South 9th East (once the rural countryside). They were members of a resilient Greek Orthodox community within a Mormon-dominated culture where dark skinned immigrants were an oppressed minority.

According to historian Helen Zeese Papanikolas,

> "Like other Mediterranean immigrants, the Greeks experienced intense discrimination. Their wages were lower than those of Americans, they were segregated on railroad gangs and often assigned the more dangerous work, and they were

prohibited from living in and buying property in certain areas."

—HELEN ZEESE PAPANIKOLAS

"THE GREEKS IN UTAH," UTAH HISTORY ENCYCLOPEDIA

While my grandparents tried to protect their family from blatant discrimination, their children often felt isolated—not protected—from the community. Each of them rebelled against my grandparents' restrictions in his or her own way.

Growing up in Utah, I knew I was different. I had dark hair and olive skin instead of blonde hair and freckles like most of my friends. Because I wanted to fit in, I decided to ignore the differences and look at the positive side of things. I rarely had to worry about sunburn like most of my friends.

I still remember the day I learned I wasn't invited to my 8-year old friend's birthday party. She lived just up the street from us on Atkin Avenue and all my friends were invited. My mother was outraged.

"You didn't get invited because you aren't Mormon. I'm going to call her mother! I know her from the PTA."

That night, I was so embarrassed I cried myself to sleep. Suddenly, I became aware of a deeper difference between my friends and me. A difference my mother knew all too well. Her father was in constant fear of KKK-inspired lynchings and violence perpetrated against Greek immigrants in Utah.

My blonde doll and me at my cousin's wedding, December 1955

I began my life as an outsider, a Greek girl, a young Gentile in a sea of Latter-Day Saints. And, like my parents and grandparents, I tried to shield my children from discrimination and prejudice. After I was married, my husband and I bought a house near the University of Utah, a religiously diverse area, and we cultivated non-Mormon friendships. Still, I'm sure my children felt a sense of being different just as I did.

~

I AM BLESSED to belong to a large, loud, loving family and to have a few close friends who have traveled with me on the long and winding road of my life, "from the West down to the East."

My mother's parents and my father's father were born in Greece. My father's mother was born in Sweden. So...

I am Greek and Swedish,

Mediterranean and Scandinavian,

Warm and cold.

In 1996, reeling from a rocky second marriage in Minnesota, my desire to better understand my own heritage led me back to Salt Lake City, Utah determined to interview each living member of my parents' generation. Inspired to learn more about myself through them, I interviewed relatives on both sides of my family who were still alive and agreed to meet with me. Only three family members on my mother's side were still alive—my mother, my Aunt Anne, and my Uncle George.

On my mother's side of the family, Wanda was the first to be buried. She was buried at Mt. Olivet Cemetery in Salt Lake City, Utah. My Aunt Wanda was a month shy of 23 years old when she died suddenly on October 16, 1948. As I write this book, she patiently guides me to a bright light at the end of a dark tunnel of grief. Small clues appear magically, seemingly out of nowhere. They show up in the treasures my mother left behind. When I least expect it, a photograph, newspaper clipping, letter, or handwritten note surfaces. One of the first photos I discovered was an oval shaped, professional wedding portrait of Wanda. It was a familiar image.

As a child, I remember visiting Grandma, Grandpa, and Wanda on Memorial Day at Mt. Olivet. We always took a bouquet of flowers to place on their graves. A large, rose colored, granite tombstone at the head of Wanda's grave featured a porcelain image of that same oval shaped portrait, a cross with grape vines gently wrapped around it, and the inscription,

DAUGHTER

WANDA W. CHAUSE

DEC 5 1924

NOV 16 1948 [sic]

The stories in HeartStrings are mine. They are based upon facts and memories, family interviews and conversations, old photographs and historical documents. My perspectives and experiences are woven into a tapestry of tales, connecting me to those who came before me and those who came after me. The stories are a celebration of our ancestors—a way to honor them and, at the same time, free our children and our children's children from the traumas of the past.

I know other family members have their own stories and I respect that. Each of us tells the stories as we know them.

THREE GENERATIONS

MY MOTHER'S GENERATION

The Chaus Family

Katina & William Chaus
My grandparents

James
(Jimmy)
1926-1974

Wanda
1924-1948

Eftihia
(Afton)
My mother
1921-2011

Alexandra
(Alice)
1920-1988

George
1919-1998

Anastasia
(Anne)
1918-2007

THREE GENERATIONS

MY MOTHER'S GENERATION

The Chaus Family

Katina & William Chaus
My grandparents

James
(Jimmy)
1926-1974

Wanda
1924-1948

Eftihia
(Afton)
My mother
1921-2011

Alexandra
(Alice)
1920-1988

George
1919-1998

Anastasia
(Anne)
1918-2007

MY GENERATION

The Kyriopoulos Family

Afton & Jim Kyriopoulos
My parents

Frank William
November 11, 1943 -
November 2, 2005

Marjorie Lin
Feb 12, 1947

Kathryn Linda
September 19, 1951

Mary Susan
August 14, 1954

Debra Ann
May 18, 1957

Jami Lee
June 4, 1960

MY CHILDREN'S GENERATION

The Kyriopoulos-Bradley Family

Marjorie Lin & Edwin James Bradley
November 24, 1968

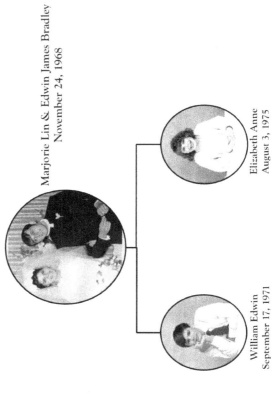

William Edwin
September 17, 1971

Elizabeth Anne
August 3, 1975

~

Bill and I met up with his friend Wes at the foot of Spanish Fork Canyon where the men prepared their guns and hunting gear. I was wearing the red sweater my mother had given me. She was determined to protect me. No way could I be mistaken for a deer! Wes led us up the side of the mountain, Bill followed him, and I trailed behind, carrying food and supplies. As we hiked deeper into the woods, there was a shuffle of dead leaves and a deer approached. Bill began loading his rifle. When I realized it was a baby deer, I tried to get his attention. I called out to him, but my voice cracked like I was in a dream. Suddenly, a bullet flew through my sweater and into my heart. In a flash, I saw my mother. She was sitting at the kitchen table, sobbing, both hands clutching her heart.

—WANDA CHAUS (CLEMENTS)

MY AUNT WANDA did not live to tell her story, so I am telling it for her – and for my grandmother, Katina Liviakis Chaus, whose heartstrings were woven into that red sweater. There are few details about the events leading up to the moment of her death, most of which appear on the front page of the October 17, 1948 edition of the Salt Lake Tribune, where a small headline reads, "Young S.L. Matron, 23, Killed in Rifle Mishap."

That night, an anonymous phone call was received at my grandparents' house. The call came just before a reporter arrived to interview the family. My Aunt Alice answered the phone. The male caller said he wanted to let her know that Wanda had been shot and her body was at the morgue. Knowing my aunt, I'm sure she hung up the phone, shocked, and let out a huge scream before she was able to tell her parents what the man had said to her.

As I imagine this scene, I am sure my grandmother broke down and cried uncontrollably, even though she was still in denial.

"No. No. No! Not Wanda. Not my baby girl!"

Wanda is buried at Mt. Olivet Cemetery in Salt Lake City, Utah, where the deer roam freely. She lies between her father and mother, William and Katina. She was their youngest daughter and the first member of my mother's family to be buried there. Wanda died in an instant, yet the grief of her untimely death is woven into three generations of my family's psyche.

About three months later, there was another phone call from an unidentified caller. This time it was a woman. Again, Alice answered the call. The caller told her that someone from the family should go to the courthouse at 9:00 am the next morning. My grandparents asked Alice to go. The next morning, when she arrived at the courthouse, she saw Wanda's husband, Bill. He was with another woman— his other wife. She was filing for a divorce. On that cold, January day, my mother's family learned the truth about Wanda's husband, the man who had disappeared from their lives months earlier. He was a bigamist.

Pandora's box opened up that day at the Salt Lake County courthouse. I was a toddler, almost two years old. As I grew older, I began to wonder about my Aunt Wanda. Why did her husband shoot her in the heart? Was she pregnant the day she died? What about Bill's "other" family? Was he a polygamist? Did the patriarchal Mormon community cover for Bill the day he shot my aunt? Did Wanda know he had another wife?

Whenever I asked my mother about my Aunt Wanda, she would respond with two simple sentences.

"It was not an accident!"

"He was already married to another woman!"

My uncle, Ernie Kyriopoulos, a WWII veteran, said to me, "Margie, Wanda's husband knew how to handle a gun. He served in the army during World War II."

It's true. According to his military record, my aunt's husband fought the battles of Normandy, Northern France, Rhineland, and Central Europe. His service was terminated on November 16, 1945 and he was decorated with a Good Conduct medal as well as a Victory Medal.

Wanda's husband Bill is the only one who knows the truth about what happened that night. Yet, that traumatic event instantly changed lives on both sides of the family— for generations. My aunt's untimely death left an emotional strain on the entire family. It was as though each of them had been pulled into the undertow as they moved through the various stages of grief—denial, anger, bargaining, depression, and perhaps for some, acceptance.

I feel Wanda's presence now more than ever. She is my muse, my Guardian Angel, my connection to the family I knew growing up. I'm sure the Deer Hunting Mishap was always there in the background, playing out my family's collective grief—my grandmother's "broken heart," my uncle's long conversations with the trees, my aunt's obsession with married men, my brilliant cousin's schizophrenia, my 5-year postpartum depression, my young cousin's sudden suicide, my mother's eyes...

MY MOTHER'S EYES

I'll always remember my mother's eyes—
the way she squints
even when she smiles,
like she's angry at the world
for all the pain that pushed its way into her heart.

Did giving birth
to an Elvis impersonator and five strong women
take its toll on her eyes, "windows to her soul?"

Did being married to my father,
a man with a million plans
and a knack for executing them,
one at a time,
put that worry in her eyes?

Did the death of her sister, Wanda,
shot in the heart by her husband,
in a "deer hunting mishap,"
work its way into her psyche?

Did she inherit the pain in her eyes
from her mother and father
who brought it with them
from El Greco?"

I see my mother's eyes in my sisters' eyes,
my brother's eyes, and mine.
Sometimes I see her eyes
in the eyes of my children,

my sibling's children,
and her great grandchildren.

My mother's eyes
are an heirloom we carry with us,
a genealogical gem – as hard to penetrate
and precious as the sapphire stone
in her mother's wedding ring,
the one I now wear
every day.

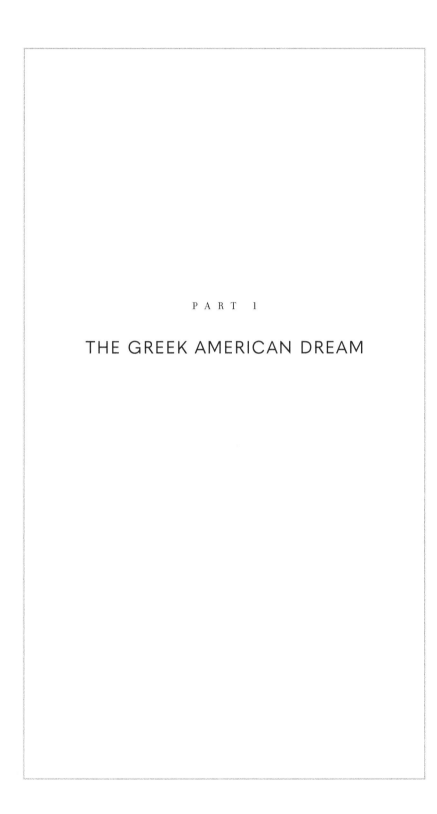

PART 1

THE GREEK AMERICAN DREAM

MY GRANDPARENTS

~

William and Katina Chaus, May 1916

I SEE MY grandparents mostly through my mother's eyes and in photographs stashed away in boxes. My mother had a deep respect for her parents. I remember sitting with her at the assisted living center in

McHenry, Illinois, where she moved in her late 80s to be closer to Jami, her youngest child.

"Margie, my mother was a wonderful woman," said Mom as she looked up at this photograph. "She was sweet and strong at the same time."

I was only three years old when my grandmother died, so I have more vivid memories of my grandfather, who was a small man with a big presence. Grandpa Chaus was the only man my mother both feared and respected.

I CAN'T GIVE YOU
ANYTHING BUT LOVE

∼

WHEN GEORGE LIVIAKIS and his brother John came to America, they landed in Pocatello, Idaho where they worked as laborers on the railroad. George arrived in 1908 and John followed him five years later. To supplement their income and send money back home to their family in Crete, the brothers bought a boarding house.

Their plan was to bring their sister, Katina, to Pocatello so she could help them out at the boarding house—cooking and cleaning—and eventually marry a wealthy immigrant from Crete. Young Katina made the long journey from Perivolia, her tiny village full of olive groves, in 1915. She was almost 23 years old, the same age as Wanda, her youngest daughter, on the day she took that short drive to Spanish Fork Canyon.

A year later, my grandmother met the love of her life:

> The day I met Vasili [William], there was no turning back. I had just finished cleaning his room when I opened the door to the hallway and there he was, tired and sweaty after working all night on the railroad tracks. "Γεια σου! (Hello)," he said, his whole body smiling back at me with those shining aquamarine eyes. They lit up the dark hallway and brightened my day, reminding me of the Mediterranean Sea back home. I think

I said hello, but all I remember is this: I couldn't wait to see him again.

As it turned out, it was love at first sight for both of us. My brothers were not happy. One Sunday after church, we were sitting together in the dining room having lunch, reminiscing about our life back in Greece and telling stories about our parents, who were still in Chania. William was in the parlor playing cards with the other men.

"Mother would approve of Vasili," I said.

"Katina, are you crazy? That guy is a lazy chain-smoking card player. To top it off, he is a 'xeno' (outsider)—he's not even Cretan," said my brother George.

"Λοιπόν, τουλάχιστον είναι Έλληνας (Well, at least he's Greek)!" I insisted.

"I'll tell you what I'm going to do," said John. I'm going to buy a gun and do him in!"

I knew he was joking, but trying to convince my brothers was like rolling a rock up the hill. Still, I persisted.

William was a simple young man from Stómion, not far from Athens. I'd never met anyone from the Peloponnese. He told me how much he loved his mother. She died when he was just a teenager and his father re-married. None of the children were happy with their new stepmother.

"I was 18 years old when I decided to come to America. I was afraid of being drafted into the Greek army and ready to start a new life in a new country," he told me.

The day he asked me to marry him was a Sunday. We were having a cup of coffee at the boarding house, engaged in another long conversation after church. That Sunday was different. I could tell he was nervous. There he was, dressed in his finest black suit and wearing a dark blue tie. Every dark brown hair on his head was in its place.

We were the only two people in the dining room, so it was unusually quiet. The floral wallpaper bounced off the sunlight and I felt like we were sitting in a garden full of bright peonies, roses, and purple irises. Then I noticed a little box in his hand. He opened it up and handed me the most unique ring I had ever seen. It was beautiful, yet simple.

"Katina, θα με παντρευτείς (Will you marry me)?" he asked. I had this ring made because it reminds me of you."

In the middle of the ring was an oval-shaped, sapphire blue Cabochon stone with two tiny rubies, one on each side. The three stones were set in a thin gold band designed with hand-carved vines winding up to the stones.

I wanted to jump up and down, but I didn't want to ruin the happiest moment of my life. I knew I'd have to convince my brothers to let me marry him.

"Ναί! (Yes, yes)," I said softly.

—KATINA LIVIAKIS (MY GRANDMOTHER)

Katina's brother John did buy a gun, but instead of doing away with William, he and George finally agreed to let Katina marry William. Although they accepted my grandfather into the family, they weren't celebrating.

My grandparents were married on May 25, 1916 at the Assumption of The Blessed Virgin Mary Greek Orthodox Church in Pocatello Idaho. It wasn't a "Big Fat Greek Wedding," but it was the perfect wedding for them—a simple ceremony in the middle of the week, on William's day off.

"Bless this marriage and grant unto these Your servants, Vasili and Katina, a peaceful life, length of days, chastity, love for one another in a bond of peace, offspring longlived, fair fame by reason of their children, and a crown of glory that

does not fade away. Account them worthy to see their children's children. Keep their wedlock safe against every hostile
scheme; give them of the dew from the Heavens above, and of
the fatness of the earth. Fill their houses with bountiful food,
and with every good thing..."

And,

"Let them behold their children's children as newly planted
olive branchlets round about their table; and, being accepted
before You, let them shine as stars in the Heavens, in You, our
Lord, to Whom are due all Glory, honor, and worship as to
Your eternal Father, and Your AllHoly, Good, and Lifecreating
Spirit, both now and ever, and to the ages of ages."

I love the Crowning ceremony. I can imagine the day my grandparents were married...First, the priest places two simple handmade crowns
joined together by a ribbon on my grandfather's head, chanting three
times,

"The servant of God, Vasili, is crowned unto the handmaiden
of God, Katina, in the name of the Father, and of the Son, and
of the Holy Spirit. Amen."

Then, he places the crowns on my grandmother's head and chants
three times.

"The handmaiden of God, Katina, is crowned unto the servant
of God, Vasili, in the name of the Father, and of the Son, and
of the Holy Spirit. Amen."

Next, he chants three times, "O Lord, our God, crown them with glory and honor," switching each crown back and forth between them. Once they are joined together by the ribbon between their crowns, the priest reads from the Bible as my grandparents each sip wine from the "common cup." Finally, still joined together by the crowns and supported by their best man (Uncle John, I'm sure), they follow the priest around the table (symbolic altar of their daily life) three times to the Dance of Isaiah.

This dance of joy began my grandparents' life together. As it did for my mother and father, and for both of my husbands and me.

Back: John and George Liviakis
Front: Vasili (William) and Katina (Katherine) Chaus, Pocatello, Idaho

~

AFTER MY GRANDPARENTS married, they began their own American
Dream, a dream full of faith, hope, and love—punctuated with pain
and suffering. I can imagine the early days of their life together.

> We were not wealthy, but our love made us feel like royalty.
> We knew how to enjoy every moment together and I loved
> watching William play Blackjack. He was so smart! I felt like
> a winner myself, lucky to be his wife. One Saturday, after we
> returned from the farmer's market and were washing our
> bounty of fruits and vegetables, William shared his dream
> with me.
>
> "Katina, how do you feel about owning our own farm
> someday?"
>
> "You mean growing our own fruits and vegetables? Raising
> chickens and pigs? Just like we did back home?" I asked.
>
> "Yes. I've always wanted my own farm. If we start saving
> now, we can make it happen someday. I am sure we can."
>
> "I love the idea of having our own farm! I'll see if I can
> get more work cleaning rooms at some of the other boarding
> houses in town."
>
> I was proud to be a part of my husband's dream.

And so it was. We worked hard and saved up for our future farm in a canning jar we hid in the cupboard. William talked with the farmers at the market and learned about the best crops to grow here. Olive trees wouldn't survive the harsh winters, but apples, pears, plums, and apricots love this area.

Within a few months, I noticed my tummy was getting bigger and I was feeling nauseous most of the time. I was both excited and nervous. I didn't think anyone else would notice, but a friend of ours who was sitting next to me at church quietly whispered in my ear one Sunday.

"Katina, είστε έγκυος (Katina, are you pregnant)?"

"δεν ξέρω (I don't know)," I whispered, pretending to be oblivious to all the signs. At that moment, the thought of my mother waved over me. As soon as I was back at the boarding house, I sat down and wrote a letter to her. It was the closest thing to being with her. Later that evening when we were getting into bed, I told William about the baby. He wasn't surprised at all. He was nervous and excited. He looked at me with those amazing eyes and kissed me softly, as though he was afraid he might hurt the baby growing inside me.

"It's going to be fine, dear," he said. "I noticed you were gaining a little weight. We'll call the doctor in the morning."

This was a big time in our lives and it happened so fast!

The next day, the doctor came to examine me. He could hear the baby's heart.

"Good news! I can hear a little heartbeat in there. Your baby is due before next spring,"

We couldn't wait to tell George and John. Since our parents were still back in Greece, my brothers were our only family in the United States.

—KATINA

On March 8th, 1917, my grandmother felt the contractions coming.

"William, it's time to go to the hospital," I called out from the top of the stairway.

"Έρχομαι, αγαπη μου (I'm coming, dear)," he said, running up the stairs.

He picked up my suitcase and followed me down the stairs and outside to the front of the boarding house. We waited there together for the street car.

I couldn't wait to see my new baby. The pain of the contractions was nothing compared to the excitement of giving birth for the first time. Finally, the streetcar arrived and we were on our way. The ride to the hospital seemed like an eternity. The labor pains got closer together. Both the driver and William were nervous.

Once we arrived at the hospital, William ran in and came out with a nurse, who rushed me into the hospital. She took me past the front desk and into the maternity ward. William checked me in at the front desk, but he was not allowed in the delivery room. He had to wait in the waiting room.

—KATINA

This is the longest day of my life. First, there was the long ride in the street car and now this. Waiting, waiting, waiting with all the other fathers. I am not down on my knees but I am praying to you, God. Please protect my wife and our new baby.

—WILLIAM DEMITRIUS CHAUS (MY GRANDFATHER)

William and Katina's first child, William Jr., was born that day, silently. We don't have any details about what happened. The death certificate reads, simply, "Still born." I can imagine my grandfather's shock when the doctors told him the news. I can imagine my grandmother, crying herself to sleep in the hospital while all the other mothers were feeding their babies. Postpartum depression must be an even deeper blue without the joy and unconditional love of a new baby in your arms as the milk flows freely from your breasts. Katina's heartstrings were stretched thin that day.

KATINA KNOWS THINGS

∾

THE TRAGIC LOSS of their first child brought my grandparents closer
together. They began a Memorial Day tradition that became a family
tradition for future generations. A visit to the cemetery followed by a
memorial lunch.

Our first child will always have a place in our hearts, especially
today. It's Memorial Day and Katina is cooking a chicken to
take on our picnic. First, she washes the chicken. Then, she
rubs it with a mixture of olive oil, lemon juice, and oregano
and puts it into the pan with freshly peeled carrots and Idaho
potato wedges. Next, she pours the rest of the lemony olive oil
over the potatoes.

We're planning to take the streetcar to Blackrock Canyon
with George and John to enjoy a picnic lunch together. Spring
is my favorite season. The hills are blooming with colorful
wildflowers. Katina's favorites are the bright yellow daisies.
They remind her of the dandelions back home. She will pick
a few to place on baby Billy's gravesite on the way back to the
boarding house.

I'm getting used to the family's Cretan ways. Living in
Crete, an island the Turks love to invade, made them independent and strong. Even the women. My wife is one of the

strongest women I know. I love her quiet strength. I am the man of the house, yet she knows I am not as strong as she is. We don't even have a house. We're still living in her brothers' boarding house with a bunch of immigrant men, saving our money for the farm.

"Katina," can I help you?"

"Οχι (No), Thank you. I'm almost ready. Well, maybe you could help me. Would you put the plates, napkins, and silverware into the picnic basket?"

Katina is a classic. She always uses her mother's china and silverware, even for a picnic. It's her way of being close to her mother. I know that feeling. Especially since my mother is gone. I feel Mama's presence often, even though she's been gone for years. It's as if she's standing there next to me, guiding me with her gentle voice.

I walk over to the buffet and pick out Katina's favorite napkins, the white ones she embroidered with our initials—K and V. Then I take out four plates and the silverware. As soon as I pack them into the picnic basket, George and John walk in.

"Τι μαγειρεύει; (What's cooking?). Smells like Katina's famous lemon oregano chicken!" Says John as he and George sit down at the table.

"Ναι, είναι κοτόπουλο (Yes, it's chicken)!" It's almost ready," says Katina.

I sit down next to my brother-in-law. Out of the blue, George asks me a question I didn't expect. Then again, you never know what the brothers will come up with next.

"Vasili, could you and Katina manage this place until we sell it? John and I are tired of working on the railroad. We want to move west and look for jobs working in the mines."

"Ναί, φυσικά (Yes, of course) we can help you. Let's talk

about it over lunch. Some of the men at the railroad moved to Utah a few months ago. Maybe there's a lot of opportunity there."

Katina told me later she already had an intuition about her brothers' plan. She's like that. A quiet wife who always seems to know things.

—WILLIAM

Within a month, John and George were gone. George moved to Clarkdale, Arizona and John moved to Price, Utah. Both of them found jobs working in the mines. My grandparents managed the boarding house and my grandfather continued working on the railroad.

When the new buyers took over the boarding house in the fall, William and Katina decided to move to Utah. They packed up all their belongings and took the train to Salt Lake City. Once they arrived, John helped them find an apartment downtown near the Greek community.

My grandmother was happy to be living closer to her family. She and my grandfather were still saving their money to buy a farm and, she was pregnant again. William was able to find a job at Union Pacific Railroad in Utah and Katina found work cleaning houses. They were still saving up to buy a farm.

When I returned from work on January 31ˢᵗ, Katina was waiting for me with her bag packed.

"It's time, Vasili. The baby is coming," she said, calmly.

"Ας πάμε τώρα (Let's go now)" I said, praying for it to be different this time. We made it to the hospital just in time. Both of us were anxious, but the nurse and the doctor assured us that everything was fine.

"The baby is in the right position and I can hear a strong heartbeat," said the doctor.

Again, I waited outside the delivery room. This time, I was more anxious, but hopeful. I called John from the hospital.

"John, I just want to let you know we are at the hospital. Katina is in labor."

"Thank you for letting me know, Vasili. I'm praying for you both," he said.

Suddenly, I heard a baby's cry and I couldn't help myself. I cried too. The doctor came out and congratulated me. The baby was alive! It was a girl! We had already decided on the name Anastasia if it was a girl. The doctor walked with me to the delivery room and there was Katina, holding our little Anastasia and smiling up at me, tears of joy running down her face.

—WILLIAM

Just six months later, my grandmother had a premonition. She knew something was wrong. Immediately, she wondered about her brothers.

It was early in the morning and Katina was awake, breastfeeding little Anastasia, when she whispered in my ear.

"Wherever I go, I smell the Livani (incense)."

"Hmmm. I can't smell anything. Maybe you were dreaming with your nose," I joked.

We went back to sleep, but she tossed around in bed all night long.

"Vasili, not only did I smell the Livani, I also heard a rooster crow three times last night. I didn't want to wake you up, but I'm worried."

"Okay. I'll go outside and check to see if a stray rooster made its way into the chicken coop."

I went outside to check it out and came back inside.

"There is no rooster, Katina," I assured her. Yet Katina knew something bad had happened. She just knew things.

"Vasili," she said, with that worried look on her face. "Will you call my brothers? I want to make sure they are okay?"

"Sure," I said. I called George first. No answer. Then, I called John and he answered the phone.

"I'm fine, Bill," said John. "How is my sister? And how's little Anastasia?

"They are both fine. Thank you, John. Katina heard a Rooster crowing last night and she smelled the incense. You know how sensitive she is."

"That's my sister. I'll call George and get back to you as soon as I hear from him," he promised. A few hours later, John called back. His voice was shaking.

"Bill, there's been an accident. George was floating down the river on a raft and something happened. The river took him over. I can't believe it. Bill, he's gone. I should tell Katina myself."

"Yes. I think that would be best," I said. I put down the receiver and went into the bedroom where Katina was changing the baby's diaper.

"Katina, it's John. He wants to talk with you. I'll hold the baby."

I picked up little Anastasia and sat in the rocking chair. Katina walked into the kitchen and picked up the phone.

"Hello, John." At first, she was silent. Then, she began to sob uncontrollably.

"Όχι, όχι, όχι (No, no, no). Όχι Γιώργος (Not George!)"

Katina was in shock. I put Anastasia in her cradle and rushed over to the kitchen to comfort my sweet Katina. As I held her in my arms, she dropped the receiver and I picked it up. John was still talking.

"I'm going to Arizona now."

"It's me....Vasili," I said.

"Okay. I know this is difficult for Katina. I'll call you as soon as I know more. Take care of my sister."

"I promise, John. I'm so sorry. May his memory be eternal."

Katina walked into the bedroom and fell onto the bed. She was unable to move. I lay down next to her, held her in my arms, and let her cry herself to sleep.

—WILLIAM

Perhaps the rough rapids on an early summer day carried my grandmother's brother away. When the water is high on the river, rapids can take control of a raft or boat, even if the boater is experienced.

There is a photograph of George Liviakis's funeral in 1918 in a book written by my mother's cousin. It's a strange photograph. George is in a closed casket, propped up on the front steps of the Greek Orthodox church. The casket is surrounded by family and friends posing for the photographer.

A bearded Greek priest in his finest robes holds up the casket. There are flowers on the casket and wreaths propped up on both sides of the casket at the bottom of the stairs. My grandmother stands on his right, wearing all black with a black kerchief over her head. She is bowing down with her whole body, visibly shaken as she mourns her brother's death, her heartstrings stretched thin again. Her brother John is behind her, holding her arm as if to save her from a fall. My grandfather stands on the priest's left, his head bowed in prayer.

I know this church well—Holy Trinity Greek Orthodox Church, 279 South 300 West, Salt Lake City, Utah. It is the church where my father's parents were married in 1907, the church where my parents were married in 1942, the church where I went to Sunday School growing up, and the church where my husband and I were married in 1968.

THE EARLY YEARS

~

MY GRANDPARENTS WERE true lovebirds. They didn't waste any time starting a family once they moved to Utah. Within three years, four healthy children were born—Anastasia, George, Alexandra, and Eftichia (my mother).

Almost a year after my mother was born, my grandmother was in labor again. It was early in the morning of December 22, 1922. This time, it was an emergency. For some reason, my grandfather ran down the road to find a doctor. Was it someone they knew? Had they heard there was a doctor in the neighborhood? I'm not sure why, but he found a doctor down the street.

"Katina, this man is a doctor. He can help us."

Vasili was out of breath and a bit anxious. I looked up at the doctor. He was tall, thin, and blonde. He was wearing a white shirt and suspenders.

"Hello Katina," he said. He asked Vasili to boil some water and find some clean towels. Then, he examined me.

"Katina, can you relax and try to breathe deeply?" he asked.

Relax? I thought. Something was wrong. I just knew it.

"I'll try," I said, tears beginning to stream down my face. I thought about little Billy, our first baby, buried in Pocatello. I moaned and cried and called for Vasili who was busy trying to help the doctor and manage the children at the same time. The girls were playing together and George was watching over little Effie.

"Push, Katina. It's time to push." I pushed as hard as I could, but the baby wasn't coming. Something was wrong. We looked up at the doctor. He was speechless. The look on his face made me realize he knew something was wrong too. Finally, he found his voice.

"Katina. I'm afraid we need to get you to the hospital," he said softly. Then he said something about the umbilical cord. I didn't understand what he said. "I can drive you there. Your husband and the children can follow us."

All I knew was that we had to get to the hospital. My English is so bad. I pulled on my house dress and waddled out to the car, holding on to the doctor. As he drove me to Holy Cross Hospital, he was deep in thought. Once we got to the hospital, a nurse came out with a wheelchair. I looked at the clock. It was 9:00. Friday morning.

"Hello, Katina. I'm Freda," she said. "Let's get you into a room." Freda was young and kind. She helped me up onto a bed and gave me a glass of water.

"The doctor will be in shortly."

"Thank you," I said, confused.

Another doctor came into the room with the doctor who drove me to the hospital. I knew my baby was still inside me. The new doctor checked for the baby's heartbeat and examined me. Then, both doctors looked at each other silently.

"Katina," said the new doctor. "I'm afraid your baby's umbilical cord was in the wrong position during labor and the baby lost oxygen."

I burst into tears just as Vasili walked into the room.

"Katina, are you alright? The nurse is watching the children. "Where is the baby?"

"The baby is still inside me," I sobbed.

"I'm so sorry," said the second doctor. "I'm afraid your baby did not survive."

My baby was gone. Just like our first baby boy. And my heart was broken again. I slid down and covered my face with the sheet, sobbing.

—KATINA

"Infant Chaus," a baby boy, was born and died on the same day at Holy Cross Hospital at 11:00 am. Cause of death: "Prolapse of umbilical cord before birth. Still Born." The neighborhood doctor never forgot what had happened that night. He came to visit the family often. Every time he visited, he paced the floor, back and forth.

"Tell me more about your religion. I want to know more," he said. In a strange way, his visits helped me heal.

"The Greek Orthodox Church was the first Christian church," I said in my broken English. "It goes back as far as the 12 Apostles. Would you like to come to church with us some Sunday?"

"Maybe so. I'll let you know."

The good doctor never came to church with us. When he stopped visiting us, we wondered why. Then, one day, a neighbor stopped by with news about the neighborhood doctor.

"Katina, the doctor is gone. He took his own life. The neighbors all believe he could no longer live with himself after what happened to your baby."

"ω Θεέ μου (Oh, my God)! I'm so sorry." I said. In my heart, I said a little memorial prayer for him. *"May his memory be eternal."*

We never blamed the doctor, but he blamed himself. We were both so sad to hear the news.

—KATINA

My grandparents later learned the neighborhood doctor was not an obstetrician. No wonder he felt so responsible for what happened to their tiny baby boy. Still, he was a doctor. And he was just one man. Today, babies are born with the help of an entire support team, specialists, and state-of-the-art equipment.

A little over a year later, Wanda was born and Katina was ecstatic. She had gone through a long year of loss after her previous painful pregnancy so she knew Wanda was a gift from God.

My grandparents were still saving up for their farm, hoping for a new start of their own. Meanwhile, Katina's brother, John, was still working at the Castle Gate Mine in Carbon County.

Life in America for my grandparents' family, as for most immigrants, was unpredictable. On March 8, 1924, Uncle John stayed home from work to care for his wife who was ill. Because he was home, he escaped a tragedy that unfolded at the mine that day during a series of three explosions. All 171 workers were killed. All were immigrants—50 Greeks, 25 Italians, 32 Englishmen or Scots, 12 Welsh, four Japanese, and three Austrians (or South Slavs). John never went back to the mine. He and his family packed up and moved to Sacramento, California. Although Katina missed her brother, she was grateful he was not at work that day.

Finally, during the 1930s, William and Katina bought a twenty-acre farm with a small farmhouse—too small for their family of eight, but it had potential. The first big project was to build a larger house next door. Both Aunt Anne and my mother shared some memories of life on the farm with me.

He was a neat guy. I loved my father. But he was also stern as a parent. When Dad said something, you'd better listen.

Life was difficult back then. Farming was Dad's passion, but he had a difficult time selling his bounty in the city. Mormon farmers were given prime spots at the Farmer's Market, so they always sold more produce than we did.

We all worked on the farm when we were kids. We worked in the vegetable garden hoeing, thinning, and topping the sugar beets and we milked the cows every day so mother could make butter and cheese. I remember how we used to have milk fights in the barn, squirting each other as we milked the cows. We knew how to have fun on the farm. We also knew we had to follow dad's rules.

Eventually, Dad had to go back to work on the railroad. He was so disappointed in himself that he wasn't able to live out his dream. And none of us wanted to stay around to work on the farm once we got older. It was especially difficult for my brother George. He never wanted to be a farmer and he couldn't wait to leave home.

—ANNE CHAUS STONE

I can't imagine giving birth to a child every year. Or delivering a still born baby. I can't imagine raising six children either. My grandfather's dream was for his children to take over the farm. That's how it all began. The day my grandparents bought the farm, their older children were able to work the crops, feed the animals, and sell his bounty at the market.

My mother and father were loving and caring parents with a lot of worries. You could tell they had money problems, but they didn't let that bring them down. They were both small people and very good looking! Dad had blue-green eyes and was a spunky guy. Mom was a good mother. She always took good care of us kids. We raised our own food—vegetables, fruit trees, chickens, turkeys, and rabbits. We had goats and cows for milk and cheese. The kids all helped out, pulling weeds, thinning the vegetables, and taking care of the animals.

Our farm house had a big front porch and a small back entrance. In the heat of the day, we often took time out as a family in the shade of the backyard, drinking water from the well and sitting on the swing or chairs after a few hours of working on the farm. My mother grew beautiful pink Peonies, white Tulips, bright yellow Day Lilies, and Gerber Daisies. The garden brightened our long, hard working days on the farm.

—AFTON CHAUS KYRIOPOULOS

The Chaus Family in Salt Lake County, Circa 1935
My grandparents William (1888-1958) & Katina (Katherine) Chaus (1893-1950)
with their six children: George, Anastasia (Anne), Alexandra (Alice), Eftichia
(Afton), Wanda, & James (Jimmy)

Photographs of my grandparents during the early years on the farm show them beaming with pride, happy to be living the Greek American dream. Unlike the couple in Grant Wood's painting, *American Gothic*, I imagine my grandfather wearing blue denim overalls, smiling. My grandmother stands beside him, her dark brown hair pulled back in a bun.

There is a family story about a day when one of their male friends came to visit.

> One day, when William was out working on the farm, our friend was visiting. I made him a cup of coffee and offered him some Koulourakia. We had a nice conversation and I told him all about our plans for the house next door. All of a sudden, it got so quiet I could hear the wind blowing through the corn husks. I looked over at him and then I wished I had looked out the window instead.
>
> "Katina, why don't you run away with me."
>
> "What? Why would I do that? I am married to the man I love!"
>
> I was shocked. What was he thinking?
>
> "I would never leave my husband! We are still as much in love as we were the day we met."
>
> —KATINA

According to my mother, Katina had a kind heart—and she was always right.

One day, in the early 1970s, my mother and I were going somewhere in my car with baby Bill in the back, strapped in to his not-so-safe car seat. Mom was trying to give me some parenting advice and her voice became so high pitched, she was yelling at me. Thanks to my therapy sessions, I gathered up enough strength to calmly ask her a simple question.

"Mom, I'm right here. Next to you."

Then, a few minutes later, I asked, "I'm just wondering, did your mother yell at you a lot?"

No response. Mom was suddenly silent. She was silent for days on that topic. About a week later, I received a phone call.

"Hello."

"Margie," said my mother, "I just want to let you know that... yes... sometimes my mother did raise her voice...but she was always right!"

"I'm sure she was," I replied, and we continued our mother-daughter talk.

I smile inside as I recall how I tried my best to accept her outbursts without responding in kind. Now that my own children are adults, I sometimes find myself unconsciously engaging in the same mother-knows-best interactions. It's a pattern I obviously inherited years before I was aware it was happening.

Some days, I am my mother.

~

IN MY MOTHER'S family, being right and being in control were charac-
ter traits established over time, through life's lessons. Grandma Chaus
was always right and Grandpa Chaus was always in control. Or so it
seemed.

Grandpa was the disciplinarian, determined to follow Greek traditions (including arranged marriages) even though he and Grandma fell
in love in Idaho and arranged their own marriage. All of the children
spoke English better than their parents and the girls loved the American
lifestyle—dating, dancing, and socializing with friends.

> By the time I was 15 or 16, my mom and dad started trying
> to find a husband for me, but it wasn't working out very well.
> There was one guy who came over and said he wanted to
> marry Alice because she was more aggressive.
>
> "No, we've got to marry Anne off first," said my parents.
>
> I said no anyway. I said no to all of them. God, they had
> about three or four men come to see me back then.
>
> I ended up working in the evenings for Mr. Neilson, a
> music teacher. My pay covered the cost of clarinet lessons for
> George and violin lessons for Afton. I went with Mr. Neilson
> to his students' homes, collected money for the lessons, and

then he took me home after all the music lessons. My mother began to wonder whether I was in love with him.

"I do love him," I said, "like a father."

"We are still worried about you, Anne. We told Mr. Neilson you could no longer work for him."

After that, I got so depressed. I had no idea what was going to happen to me. I was the oldest child and the oldest daughter. It was a hard time for me and I didn't like the old ways, so it was hard for me growing up.

—ANNE

Grandpa and Grandma were worried about Anne. It wasn't enough just to remove her from the job. They sent my Aunt Anne off to Sacramento to live with Grandma's brother John and his wife Pelagia. That move was a turning point in her life.

They sent me to Sacramento to live with Uncle John and his wife. It was the worst time of my life! I went to school there for about a year and then I got really homesick. I didn't want to stay there any longer, but I didn't say anything.

One day, I met a boy at school who asked me to go out with him. He came to pick me up and my uncle opened the door. The boy introduced himself to my uncle and asked for me.

"Οχι (No)," said Uncle John. Then he sent the boy away.

Four years was enough for me to PUKE! My aunt and uncle thought the worst right off the bat! I was like a prisoner in their place, even though they were good to me. Eventually, I became so despondent I refused to eat and I lost my period. Just plain lost it. I'll never know how they knew. Maybe they wondered why I wasn't asking for those pads.

"Anne, where have you been? What have you been doing?" Uncle John asked me the same questions every day.

I hadn't done a doggone thing. They just kept badgering me and I had no idea what they were talking about. No idea at all. Finally, my aunt and uncle took me to a doctor to "check me out." That hurt me more than anything else. When we got to the doctor's office, the three of us waited together in silence. I stared at the white walls in the waiting room wishing I were home with my mother.

The nurse took me into a room alone. She handed me a blue hospital gown, said to put it on, and asked me to lie down on a narrow table covered with a bed sheet. A few minutes later, the doctor came in and examined me. I had never had that kind of exam with my feet up in stirrups. It was weird. And the instrument was freezing cold. I was embarrassed and the doctor seemed to be embarrassed, too.

After the exam, he washed his hands again and moved toward the door.

"Anne, you can get dressed now. I'll meet you out in the waiting room with your aunt and uncle."

I got dressed and made my way to the waiting room. The doctor was sitting there with Uncle John and Aunt Pelagia.

"This young girl is still a virgin. She is anemic and she's lost a lot of blood, so her body is reacting by stopping her menstrual cycles. Otherwise, she is a healthy young woman. I will prescribe some iron pills and you need to make sure she eats regular meals."

Thank God, the doctor had just confirmed my innocence. I mean, how did they expect me to get pregnant? They wouldn't even let me go out on a date!

Pretty soon, my sister, Afton, arrived. She had fallen in love with a young man named Jack so my parents sent her to California as well. We both got jobs working at the Cannery. I remember buying my first dress. It was so pretty with yellow and pink flowers. I also bought a beautiful, navy blue, lacy dress. I have always loved pretty clothes!

—ANNE

My mother didn't go into any of the details about living in Sacramento with her Uncle John's family. I learned more about that from Aunt Anne. The two sisters clearly had different memories of their lives growing up on the farm. As I look through all the old photos in the box of my mother's treasures, I find a snapshot of Aunt Anne, my mother, and their cousin Michael Liviakis. They are on a ferry in the San Francisco Bay. It looks like a rainy day but I see the hills in the distance. The three of them are in their late teens, early 20s. Anne and my mother are wearing stylish, double breasted coats and trendy hats. They are sitting, legs crossed, next to their cousin, Michael, who is dashing in his fashionable dark suit and tie. The three of them are smiling as they embark on a short trip across the Bay to San Francisco.

Anne, Afton, and Cousin Michael on the Ferry in the San Francisco Bay

I took that same ferry ride in 1968 when I was 21 years old, barely an adult. My memories of spending a summer in San Francisco, like my Aunt Anne's memories, are full of mixed, adult-becoming emotions.

PART 2

MY MOTHER'S GENERATION

~

Anne, Afton, Wanda, and Alice, circa 1945

THIS PHOTO OF my mother and her sisters was taken before I was born.
I believe my father was the photographer. There is happiness in the air.
The war is over and the men in their lives are coming back home. Don't

these sisters look like the happiest women in the world? Two of them are married, the other two are in love with married men, and all of their lives are about to get more complicated. I understand how this can happen. I made some pretty bad decisions myself.

SECRETS AND LIES
IN SALT LAKE CITY

~

WHEN IT CAME to love, my mother's sisters—Alice, Anne, and Wanda—followed in my grandmother's footsteps. They fell in love with and married "outsiders."

Alice met Ernie, her first husband, at the Farmer's Market in Salt Lake City where she and Uncle George spent weekends selling produce from Grandpa's garden.

One Saturday morning after George and I arrived at the market, I noticed a handsome young man out of the corner of my eye. He was watching me. I waited for a few minutes before I went up to him and introduced myself.

"Hello! My name is Alice. I'm working here for my father."

"Hi there, Alice. My name is Ernie," he said, almost laughing. "I drive a produce truck for my uncle."

"What a coincidence! I'm here with my brother. We're selling our father's bounty."

After that day, there was no turning back. We fell in love between rows of shiny red tomatoes, bright green zucchinis, and deep purple eggplants. I melted inside every time I saw him standing there, helping the customers at his uncle's produce stand. I knew better than to tell my parents about him after watching them send my sisters off to California.

It didn't take long to figure out a way to see each other behind our parents' backs. We started meeting at Snelgrove's Ice Cream Parlor downtown every Saturday after the market closed. I told my parents I was going to meet one of my girlfriends. Ernie was always there, waiting for me at the counter with a vanilla malt and two straws. Chocolate was his favorite, but he knew mine was vanilla. He was so thoughtful. Plus, we always had a ball together! He liked that I wasn't afraid to say what I thought and I liked that he was such a gentleman.

When I found out Ernie was from a good Mormon family, I thought, "Boy, my father would be even more upset with me if he found out about us. He'd heard too many stories about the Klu Klux Klan-inspired cross burning protests against mixed marriages between Greeks and Mormons."

No matter what, Ernie and I were determined to make it work. One bright Spring Friday afternoon, we were strolling around Pioneer Park and we found a park bench underneath a flowering cherry blossom tree. We sat on the bench and looked into each other's eyes. He held my hand and we kissed each other. At that moment, I didn't have a care in the world. I was just happy to be on that park bench with him.

"I need to tell you something, Alice," he said, hesitating.

"What is it? Is something wrong?"

"Well, nothing's wrong with us," he said. "Something is wrong with the world. I need to leave for the army in a few days."

Suddenly, the clouds moved in and the sky grew darker. I felt a chill in my bones and I started to shiver. Tears welled up inside and I wanted to scream.

Ernie held me closer.

"I have an idea. Let's get married tomorrow morning. It's a Sunday, so you can tell your parents you want to go to your friend's house after church. Then, we'll drive to Nevada and get married."

"What? Are you serious?"

"Absolutely. We can tell our parents after I get back from the war. No one needs to know about it yet. We've kept it a secret until now anyway. I love you and I want to be with you for the rest of my life. Who knows what the future will bring?"

I could see the two of us, driving through the boring Nevada desert together. The thrill of a secret adventure was sure to make it an exciting trip.

"What a brilliant idea! I love you, Ernie. Let's do it!"

We kissed again and it was like we were already married. I couldn't wait to make it official. When I opened my eyes, the sun was shining again and I saw a double rainbow in the sky. I was sure it was a sign.

—ALICE CHAUS

So began the family tradition of secrets and lies.

In the early spring of 1942, Ernie and Alice were married at a Wedding Chapel in Elko, just days before Ernie left for his tour of duty with the Coast Artillery Corps. After they were married, they drove straight back to Utah and Alice went home that night as though nothing out of the ordinary had happened. She lived with her parents while Ernie was in training and neither of them said a word about their clandestine marriage.

Their secret didn't last long though. The love birds finally revealed the truth about their Nevada marriage when Ernie was back home on a furlough a few months later. My grandparents were not happy about the union. Nevertheless, they insisted on a church wedding.

I can imagine the conversation between Katina and her daughter...

"Alexandra, I've already talked with the priest. You and Ernie need to get married in the church while he is home."
"Oh, that would be wonderful, Mama!"

Even though Ernie was a Mormon, he was able to marry my aunt in the Greek Church, which is not allowed today unless he were to become an Orthodox Christian. Tradition is important in our family, so I'm sure my grandmother made it happen somehow.

In their wedding photo, Alice is wearing a long, flowing wedding gown. She's holding a huge bouquet of roses and ferns. Ernie's hand rests on her shoulder as they pose in front of Holy Trinity Greek Orthodox Church and parishioners in the background bear witness to the happy young couple.

Alice and Ernie Hale, Holy Trinity Greek Orthodox Church, circa 1942

Against the backdrop of WWII, I imagine this "mixed marriage" was actually a pleasant distraction for my grandparents. By then, they had two sons and two sons-in-law at risk of being killed at war. Briefly, the family could stop thinking about the war and celebrate love.

HAPPINESS

~

EFTICHIA MEANS HAPPINESS—One who cares about the happiness and well-being of others around her. My mother, whose Greek name was Eftichia, was a beautiful woman with shiny, dark brown hair and a contagious smile. As a young girl, she hated her nickname, Effie, so she decided to change her name to Afton on her first day at school. It stuck with her. From that day on, she was Afton Chaus. I wonder whether she knew Efticheia meant "Happiness" in Greek.

My mother always looked young for her age, at any age. She loved to paint her nails a shiny, bronze color and she loved yellow flowers. Every summer, when bright, yellow day lilies are in full bloom, I feel her presence all around me.

Afton was passionate about the happiness and well-being of others. A helicopter mom before her time, she hovered over her one son and five daughters like a mamma bear, despite the fact that her own life was punctuated with bouts of chronic illness, depression, disappointment, and grief.

> Sometimes, I wonder what life would have been like had I married Jack Anderson, my first true love. When my parents found out, they sent me to my Uncle John's house in California— the same place they sent Anne when she fell in love with our piano teacher. Once I came back home, I followed my parents'

wishes. I married Jim Kyriopoulos, a young Greek man whose father owned a diner and a service station across the street from Nibley Park Golf Course.

—AFTON

Jack Anderson was a journalist who later became a Pulitzer Prize-winning investigative reporter. My mother followed him in the news, especially Parade Magazine, pointing out to me that she almost married a famous journalist. Anderson was quoted by the Washington Post as having said, "I have to do daily what Woodward and Bernstein did once."

I am glad she met my father, James Theodore Kyriopoulos, who was a big man with a huge heart for his family and a fun-loving laugh. His brother, Ernie, had dated Mom, but Dad won her over with his charming personality and they were married in 1942, during WWII. Theirs was a "Big, Fat, Greek Wedding."

Afton and Jim Kyriopoulos and Wedding Party, October 4, 1942

I always wanted to please my parents. They worked hard every day and they loved America, even though they didn't speak English very well.

"William," Jim said to my dad, "I am asking your permission to marry your daughter, Eftichia."

My parents were ecstatic! There would be a big Greek wedding, whether they could afford it or not. Jim's family was also Greek. Well, his mother came here from Sweden, but she loved the Greek traditions and she was baptized in the Greek Orthodox Church when she married Jim's father. I always enjoyed his family's sense of humor. My family, having escaped war-torn Crete, was more serious.

We were married in 1942 and it was a big celebration with beautiful, handmade wedding crowns for the ceremony. After the wedding, we showered everyone with my mother's beautifully hand wrapped Koufeta (Jordan Almonds). For our honeymoon, we took a trip to Jackson Hole, Wyoming. It was Jim's family's favorite place to get away.

After the big day was over and we were able to relax in Wyoming, I felt a lot of pain in my fingers.

"Jim, I'm not sure what's happening. The joints in my fingers are all swollen and painful," I said.

"It looks like arthritis to me, Afton. Let's go to a doctor when we get back home."

So that is what we decided to do. In a strange turn of events, by the time we got home, the swelling went down and I completely forgot about it until it came back again a few months later.

Finally, we went to a doctor who diagnosed me with Rheumatoid Arthritis. By then, Jim was a mechanic in the Army Air Corps working on B-17 Bombers. He wasn't allowed to fly the airplanes because of a heart murmur from the Rheumatic Fever he had as a child.

The Army Air Corps moved us to Hobbs, New Mexico where we lived from 1942 to 1946. It was a warmer climate, so we were both hoping it would help cure my arthritis. No such luck. Then, to top it off, I got pregnant. For some reason, I was losing weight instead of gaining. I weighed about 97 pounds when my sister, Alice, came to visit us. She walked in and looked at me, amazed.

"My God, Afton! You look like you swallowed a watermelon!" she was laughing and crying at the same time. I was too.

I can still hear her voice. I did look like I had a big, round watermelon inside me! I was so skinny. And then imagine this great big stomach right here, sticking out!

It was 1943. Frank was born in November and after he was born, my arthritis got worse. All the joints on my arms and legs got swollen. Everyone was worried about me. In fact, my mother, who spoke almost no English, took the bus to New Mexico to help me care for my baby. Once she returned to Salt Lake City, she called me on the telephone.

"Eftichia, you won't believe what happened to me on my way back home! My purse was stolen. I don't even know how it happened. Anyway, I had to take the bus all the way back home with no food."

"Oh, Mamma. I'm so sorry to hear that, but so happy to hear you made it home safely."

After the war was over, we moved back to Salt Lake City and I traveled back and forth to Hobbs for treatments. It was 1946. Jim was really worried about me. He was afraid I was going to die.

"Afton," he said, "I'm not sure those treatments are helping you. In fact, you seem to be getting weaker every day. I think we should try those gold treatments the doctor mentioned."

I agreed, even though it sounded strange to me, I decided to try the experimental gold injections. I had nothing to lose and I was desperate for a cure. Magically, those gold injections did the trick. My arthritis disappeared and never returned.

—AFTON

My mother recovered just in time to get pregnant with me, her second child. I was born on February 12, 1947, the same year her sister Wanda married Bill.

Mom and Me, 1947

Margie was just a baby when we lived at 1033 East Ramona Avenue. And she was quite a baby. I'll tell you! She won first place in a beauty contest when she was just a year old. What a princess! I had a hot time with little Margie! She wouldn't take the bottle and she didn't want to nurse either. She didn't like to go to sleep and often, she had bouts of colic.

At night, Jim and I would take her for a ride in the car so she would fall asleep. Can you believe it? Frank would be in bed sound asleep and, I can't believe we did this. We didn't go far—just around the block. But we got in that rickety old Woody and drove around the block just to get her sleepy enough to take her bottle and fall asleep!

—AFTON

~

SALTAIR, A RESORT on the south side of the Great Salt Lake, was designed and built by the Mormon Church to be a family-friendly, "Coney Island of the West." It opened on Memorial Day in 1893 and was advertised as "the world's largest dance floor." The resort burnt down in 1925, but it was rebuilt and survived until it closed down again during the Great Depression.

By the 1960s, the resort was a deserted, crumbling structure on the shores of the Great Salt Lake. I remember walking along the Great Salt Lake beach in bare feet when I was a teenager. The shoreline was covered with a blanket of tiny, stinky brine shrimp and there was no escaping these crunchy creatures. Yet, once I jumped into the lake, they became a distant memory. Suddenly, I was bobbing around like a cork on the water with no particular place to go as the salty water inflicted a sharp, stinging sensation on any minor scrapes or scratches. It was a strange, healing experience.

In my version of Wanda's story, she met her future husband, Bill, on the dance floor at Saltair. Young Wanda had curly, dark brown hair and green eyes that sparkled, just like her father's. She was a beautiful, kind young woman—and a bit sassy. Growing up, her buck teeth were her most noticeable feature. William and Katina believed their daughter's teeth would eventually fix themselves, but they didn't. Once Wanda graduated from Granite High School, she got a job and saved her money until she had enough to get them fixed. Finally, her smile matched her personality.

Saltair Poster, circa 1925

It was Memorial Day, 1945. Saltair was celebrating a grand re-opening of the resort in honor of WWII Veterans. I convinced Anne to take me out dancing. She loved to dance and I was excited to go out dancing with her now that I had my new teeth! I was 20 years old and it was my first time to go out without the family.

The moment I saw Bill on the dance floor, I knew we were meant to be. He smiled at me and I smiled back. I guess I was flirting with him. Then he came over to where Anne and I were standing.

"May I have this dance?" He asked.

I looked into his deep blue eyes, the color of a perfect sky, and said, "Yes. Of course."

I took his hand, fell into his arms, and we danced all night long, until the last dance. It was love at first sight.

—WANDA

Bill was tall, handsome, blonde, and charming. He had a contagious smile. He had returned home from the war lucky to be alive, yet not so lucky in love. He and his wife were having problems and things got even more complicated when he fell in love with another woman—my Aunt Wanda.

FOOLS RUSH IN

~

ANNE HAD THE demeanor of a dumb blonde even though she was a beautiful brunette. Like Marilyn Monroe, she was determined to live life on her terms. She told me her stories and asked me to write her biography. During my interviews with her, Aunt Anne shared secrets with me that she had never told my mother, who stood in judgment against her for as long as I can remember. I wonder whether Anne spent most of her life fulfilling the prophecy of her parents' worst nightmare—that she would get pregnant before she was married.

> Our parents wanted to isolate us from outsiders and teach us the old-fashioned way, the way they grew up. It didn't work out that way and I was the worst one of the bunch. I don't care though. I am not sorry for my life. I know I did things that maybe were not right. But I did what I wanted to do. I have no regrets about anything. Nobody told me do this or do that. Lucky me. I fell in love twice—once in my twenties and again in my seventies.
>
> —ANNE

Once she was allowed to go back home after being banished to Sacramento, Anne got a job at a café as a hostess in Clearfield, Utah. The owner was a man named Tony. He was the first love of her life.

Unfortunately, he was a married man with a family. And, he was a Mormon.

I was in love with him so bad. I couldn't see anything else. My whole life revolved around him and the work I was doing over there. It's crazy, I know. He was my boss, and he was married to another woman. But that's the way it was. Then, the unthinkable happened. I got pregnant. I had no idea what to do. I was getting big, big, big. Thank God it was winter so I could wear these big, sloppy clothes. And, thank God for my sister Alice who came up with an elaborate plan for me. Not only was she smart, she knew how to keep a secret!

"Anne, you are getting too big. You can't hide it much longer. If you really want to keep this baby, you either need to tell mom and dad or you need to move out of the house," Alice said to me.

"What? Where will I go? I need to keep my job and I want to keep this baby. I'm not going to let someone else have my baby. How can I tell mama and papa I'm pregnant and the guy is married? You know what they would do. They'd send me off to California to live with Uncle John again. He's worse than Papa! Remember when I knew nothing about having babies and they sent me to live with Uncle John in California? What a waste! He and Aunt Pelagia took me to a doctor because they thought I was pregnant. Now look at me!"

"Okay. Let's think about it, Annie. What if you were to move into a hotel downtown and tell everybody Tony transferred you to another city?" she asked. "And, by the way, make sure he pays for it. He owes you!"

Brilliant idea!

I told the family my boss transferred me to California. Instead, I moved into the Carlton Hotel in downtown Salt

Lake City. Then, I wrote letters to my parents and Alice sent them to a friend of hers in Los Angeles who sent them to my parents, one by one, each week, postmarked from California. It was the perfect plan!

Every morning, I ate breakfast at the café across the street. One morning, I was sitting there, very pregnant, thinking about Tony. I went over to the jukebox and picked a song by Eddie Allen. "I'll Hold You in My Heart." Suddenly, a man called out my name. I looked up and there was Harry, Jim and Afton's brother-in-law. He was carrying a stack of records for the jukebox. That was his job. He made sure the latest hits were loaded into jukeboxes. To top it off, he worked with Alice.

"Anne?" he was obviously surprised to see me. "I thought you moved to California. What are you doing here?" His eyes moved from my face to my big fat belly, the answer to his question.

"Oh, Harry. I'm so ashamed of myself. Yes, I'm pregnant. And I don't want to tell my parents. Only Alice knows about it."

"They'll find out sooner or later, don't ya think, Anne?" he asked.

Now what was I going to do? I stood there for a moment. Speechless. Then I waddled back to the counter, tears pouring down my face.

"Harry is right," I thought. "What am I going to do after the baby comes? And now that Harry knows, sooner or later, everyone in the family will find out."

Of course. Harry told Helen who told Jim and the next time Alice came to visit, she brought Jim with her.

I begged Harry, Helen, and Jim to keep it a secret, so they

promised not to tell anyone else, including our parents and our other sisters and brothers.

I felt guilty about keeping my baby a secret from the rest of my family, but I could trust Alice. She always spoke her mind and she would never talk about me behind my back. And, Jim promised not to tell Afton. She would never understand! Afton was pregnant, too. She was about to deliver her second child. And, Wanda had her own problems with our parents. She was about to marry a Mormon!"

My baby was almost ready to come when I met a woman at the coffee shop. Her name was Grace and she was an angel. She really was. And I lied to her. I told her my husband had left me for another woman.

"Annie, you can come stay with us. Just until you get settled." Grace pleaded.

So, that's what I did. I went and stayed with Grace and her husband. She was the nicest lady. When I went into labor, Grace took me to the hospital. I ended up waiting, waiting, waiting in that daggone bed from early in the morning on Easter Sunday until midnight the next day.

While I was in labor, Jim came to the hospital and spent most of the day with me. Two months ago, Jim and Afton had been in this same hospital. Afton gave birth to their second baby, Margie. Their first child, Frankie, was already four years old. Alice and Ernie had a little girl, Kathy. She was a year old.

Here I was, expecting my first baby and I had no idea what to expect.

"Hang in there, Anne. Everything is going to be fine," said Jim calmly.

I think he was wishing the baby would die. That would solve the problem. There would be no baby and I'd go home like nothing had happened. The labor pains were getting stronger and longer. Finally, the doctor on call asked his brother to take a look at me. His brother was an obstetrician. Thank God!

"We'd better take that baby out. It's too big for her," said the obstetrician.

It was April 7th, 1947. I still remember that day like it was yesterday. They decided to do a C-section. They operated on me and pulled the baby out. It was a little boy. I was so happy to see him.

Then, suddenly, they took him away and I didn't see my baby again for eleven days. On the eleventh day, I was so upset, I cried out, "When am I going to see that daggone kid of mine?"

Finally, they brought him to me. He was a beautiful baby. I named him Richard Franklin Percell right there and then, making sure he had his Daddy's last name. I was proud and happy to be his mom. The next day, we left the hospital and went straight to Grace's house where we stayed for nine months.

Meanwhile, I was still seeing my baby's father. I loved him so much. And now we had a baby together. How could I stop seeing him? He was my baby's father.

One day, Grace put two and two together.

"Anne, you aren't married to him, are you? We really want to help you," she said.

Grace had a daughter and a son-in-law who couldn't have children of their own. And Rick was a beautiful child, so her daughter came to visit often. Grace told me she wanted to adopt my baby. She promised to let me be a big part of his life.

"You can always come and see him anytime you want to. We can give him a good life. A real good life."

The time had come. Just as Harry had predicted.

"They'll find out sooner or later. Don't ya think?"

I knew what I had to do. And the faster I did it, the better for me and for my baby. I wasn't going to give up my child. No way would I let him go. I went home and talked with my mother. I can still see her standing in the kitchen wearing her handmade flour sack apron.

"Mama, I've got a little baby."

"A μωρό (baby)? "

"Yes, I have a little baby boy."

My mother didn't say a word. She just stood there and looked at me. She was silent but her face spoke volumes. She was adding up all the months I had been gone. Finally, it all made sense.

"Well, where is he?"

"He's at my friend's house."

"Bring him home, Anastasia. We'll tell everyone we are taking care of him for someone else."

Altough I didn't like that plan, I agreed. It was the least I could do after keeping her grandson a secret for so long. When I came back home, Papa wanted to chase me out of there. He wanted me and my baby to leave. I can understand his viewpoint. He saw it as a reflection on him. But Mama was strong. She protected me.

"No, you're not going to do that to her. She's going to stay here with us and we're going to help her."

—ANNE

Anne, circa 1948

Perhaps Grace worked for an adoption agency, but Anne believed she was simply a Good Samaritan who happened to be there when she needed help. In any case, the Prodigal Daughter finally returned home with her son.

~

George, Katina, and James Chaus, circa 1945

KATINA IS HAPPY. George is back home from the war and Jimmy is home on a furlough. She will be grateful when her youngest son, Jimmy, returns home for good. They will both survive WWII alive, but both will suffer from Post-Traumatic Stress Disorder (PTSD). I remember watching my Uncle Jimmy talk to the trees while the rest of the family was gathered around the picnic table, chatting with each other.

~

"GOOD MORNING, AUNT Elaine. This is Margie, Afton's daughter. I'm in Utah and I'd love to visit with Uncle George to learn more about what it was like to grow up in the Chaus family."

"If this has anything to do with the Mormon Church, we don't want any part of it!"

"Oh no...I am Greek Orthodox—I live in Minnesota and am a member of the Greek Orthodox Church in St. Paul. I'm just here over Memorial Day and I would love to hear Uncle George's stories about growing up in the Chaus family."

No response. Elaine handed the phone over to my uncle.

"I'm not at all interested!" said Uncle George." Don't you know I recently had a stroke and I can't talk well?" He asked, his voice escalating.

"Oh, my...No. I had no idea. I'm so sorry to hear that, Uncle George," I said.

I did not know my uncle had recently suffered a stroke. How could I have known? His family had been estranged from ours since my grandfather passed away in 1958 when I was eleven years old.

"All I have to tell you is that I worked all my life. I never had a childhood. It was all work and no play. I never wanted to know anything about my parents' history. I worked all through my childhood!" my uncle said, his voice rising. "We were a poor family. We didn't have a business like your dad's family. We all worked on the farm. Just ask your mother and your aunt! They'll tell you the same thing."

Aunt Anne was a year older than George. She recalled a time when the family was sitting at the dinner table, chatting.

"Oh George, you're nuts!" She laughed, jokingly.

"When I got up from the dinner table," she said, "Dad grabbed me and slapped me hard on the cheek because I had called my brother *crazy*."

The reference to mental illness triggered an immediate reaction for my grandfather. It came from a place deep within his soul. The reference triggered a similar reaction for my mother. This reaction was epigenetic. It ran in the family.

Uncle George enlisted in the Army on June 9, 1942 and his service was terminated July 15, 1944 at Bushnell General Hospital in Brigham City, Utah. He was a Tech 5 Signal Corporal who was "honorably discharged by reason of Section II, AR 615-360." Although PTSD was real during the aftermath of World War II, it was not diagnosed as such.

Four years later, his sister Wanda was shot in the heart. Two years after that, his mother died of a broken heart. No wonder he wanted to forget about life on the farm. It was full of grief.

Although my uncle and aunt were estranged from my mother's generation, our generation is opening up the floodgates to let the love flow freely. Family reunions and get-togethers are popping up and we are sharing our stories with each other.

~

UNCLE JIMMY WAS the youngest child in my mother's family. He was 18 years old when he joined the army and he served as a PFC 1602 Mortar Gunner in 1945 and 1946. Not only did he receive an honorable discharge, Uncle Jimmy received two medals: the WWII Victory Medal and the Army of Occupation Medal.

After he was honorably discharged from the United States Army, he also struggled with what we now call Post-Traumatic Stress Disorder. Uncle Jimmy was a chain smoker who mostly kept to himself. My mom and her sisters would alternate bringing him home on Sundays. We would pick him up from the Veteran's Hospital in Salt Lake City in the morning and take him back to the hospital at the end of the day. Aunt Anne was the most loyal to Uncle Jimmy. She would bring him to family celebrations at her house where there was plenty of food and drink along with noisy family chatter. We were all gathered together for someone's birthday or to celebrate a holiday. Everyone had a grand time. As usual, I was the observer, watching my uncle as he carried on long conversations with the trees.

> I heard a rustle in the trees and asked for the pass code, but there was no response. Was it Hitler's SS sneaking up on us? Our regimen had dug in for the night and I was on guard duty after a long day of fighting. It was pitch dark, cold, and

raining. I was afraid we were being ambushed and it was my duty to shoot. So, I shot.

Horror of horrors. The approaching soldier was my commanding officer. Did he whisper the pass code because the enemy was nearby? Why didn't I hear him? Why oh why did this happen on my watch? What good is an honorable discharge when I can no longer look at myself in the mirror?

—JAMES WILLIAM CHAUS

I always wondered who Uncle Jimmy was talking with out there. Was it a flashback of the night he accidentally shot his superior during the fog of war? Was he emotionally wounded twice? Once during the war and again after he returned home and the Deer Hunting Mishap occurred? This is how I remember my uncle:

FRIEND OR FOE?

Uncle Jimmy sits alone
in a lawn chair
at the garden party,
speaking to the trees.

It's as if he's calling out
to the soldier in the woods,
"Who are you?"
"Speak, speak, speak to me."

Silence.
Something told him, "Don't shoot."
But he has his orders,
No response means

he must shoot the enemy.

It's his duty.

So he shoots the silent soldier

who, in the end, is

his friend,

his comrade,

his superior.

During the opening montage of John Huston's 1946 documentary, PMF 5019, funded by the U.S. Army, *Let There Be Light*, there is a scene where wounded soldiers are leaving a hospital ship. Those who, like my uncle, were internally wounded are the subject of his film. The film was commissioned by the government and it was kept secret until 1981. Huston's father, Walter, is the film's narrator. He opens with this phrase:

> "Here is the human salvage, the final result of all that metal and fire can do to violate mortal flesh. Some wear the badges of their pain: the crutches, the bandages, the splints. Others show no outward signs, yet they, too, are wounded."

The film includes interviews and therapy scenes of mental breakdowns.

During Vietnam, Afghanistan, and Iraq, there were no military-produced films of psychic trauma, but there were plenty of journalists working side-by-side with our troops. To this day, reporters continue to carry the message to the public through daily newspapers and magazines.

~

Wanda, November 1947

MY GRANDFATHER WAS small in stature, but he had a huge demeanor, especially when it came to his daughters. He was captain of a tight family ship. I can imagine the conversation between my grandparents about

Wanda and Bill. My grandfather was adamant. His daughter would not marry a Mormon.

> "Oχι. No! Wanda cannot go with this Mormon man! She needs to find a nice Greek man!"
>
> "Vasili, do you remember how my family reacted when we first met? They did not approve of our marriage, yet here I am, happy to be with you, my true love, a simple farmer. How can we interfere with Wanda's happiness?"
>
> I pleaded with him even though I could see his point of view. At least we are both Greek. This is different. But then, Alice and Ernie are happily married and he came from a Mormon family.
>
> —KATINA

I'm sure there were many conversations between my grandparents about Wanda. Grandma's feelings were likely as mixed as any marriage between a Mormon and a "Gentile" (non-Mormon). After all, Wanda was their youngest daughter. Anne, their oldest daughter, was still not married. It's a Greek tradition for the oldest daughter to be married first. Still, Wanda was persistent. She was blinded by her love for this charming man.

Eventually, my grandparents agreed to the marriage. On November 9, 1947, Wanda married the love of her life. It was a simple celebration at my grandparents' home. I'm sure my father was the photographer who took snapshots of the wedding couple that day as they cut a big wedding cake on the kitchen table. In one of the photos, the young couple is kissing after having read their vows at the kitchen table. There's a photo hanging on the wall behind them—a portrait of my grandparents with Anastasia, their first child. All of the wedding photos were taken inside my grandparents' home.

Bill and Wanda: Kissing the bride, November 9, 1947

There was no church ceremony, no fancy celebration, no big fat Greek wedding reception. Just a wedding cake topped with a little bride and groom on the kitchen table. Of course, a big wedding was not going to happen. As it turned out, Bill had a secret of his own. He was still married to another woman. I'm sure the family was unaware of that fact.

The young couple settled into a little apartment on Main Street. Early on, there were small signs the marriage was in trouble.

"There's more unhappiness in life than not being married," Wanda told Anne, her single parent sister.

As I tell her story, I wonder what she meant by that.

Was Bill an abusive husband? Did Wanda know he was still married to another woman? Those questions remain a mystery to this day.

~

WANDA MADE THE fateful decision to go deer hunting with her husband on October 16, 1948, a month before their first wedding anniversary. My story about what happened that night is based upon interviews with Anne and Alice, as well as the story in the Salt Lake Tribune on October 17, 1948. I also feel Wanda's presence as I tell her story.

Almost a year after we were married, Bill begged me to go deer hunting with him. I was a little nervous. I loved animals and I couldn't imagine why anyone would want to shoot a deer, even though the men in our family were all deer hunters. I tried to think of it as an adventure.

On our way out of town, we stopped at my parents' house. As soon as she saw me, my mother's face was one big smile. I was still her baby girl.

"Καλός ειλθατε, Αγάπη μου! (Welcome, my love!) We are all ready for dinner. Won't you join us?"

I could never say no to my mother, but Bill insisted we needed to get to Spanish Fork Canyon before sunset.

"Wait a minute. I'll be right back," Mama said as she ran downstairs.

She returned with a bright, red sweater in her arms, carrying it like a baby. Mama was determined to protect me from being mistaken for a deer. Her heartstrings were sewn into that sweater. I put the sweater on, buttoned it up, and promised to wear it all weekend. Then, I gave her a huge hug, kissing her on both cheeks.

"σ' αγαπώ, Mama. I love you. I'll be thinking of you all weekend."

—WANDA

My grandmother, Katina, was a soft-spoken woman with a big heart. Her love for her children was deep and pure. As she and Wanda hugged each other and said their goodbyes, Wanda whispered something in her ear. Katina didn't want to let go of her daughter. But what could she do? Wanda was a married woman. Katina stood in the doorway of the farm house, wiping away her tears and trying not to worry as she watched Wanda disappear into the distance with her husband.

Did Katina have a premonition about the drama that was about to unfold that night in Spanish Fork Canyon?

I imagine Wanda had some big news for her husband on their way to Spanish Fork Canyon.

"Honey, I have something to tell you."

"Yeah, What's that?" asked Bill.

We had been married for almost a year. Next month, we would celebrate our first anniversary. I was cautious and excited at the same time, but I had to tell him the news.

"I found out why I've been feeling sick every morning. I'm pregnant!"

"Wow! That is great news!" said Bill.

I breathed a huge sigh of relief as we drove to Spanish Fork Canyon. I had been afraid to break the news to him for weeks. He had been working late every night and I was feeling a strange distance between us. Finally, we were alone together. It was the perfect time to share the news with him.

We met his friend Wesley at the foot of the mountain where we greeted each other. Wes took the lead up the mountain. It was dusk, the perfect time for deer hunting. As we hiked deep into the woods, we heard a shuffle of dead leaves. When I realized it was a baby deer, I called out to Bill. I wanted to let him know the deer was a baby.

—WANDA

At that moment, according to the Salt Lake Tribune,

"Mr. Clements began throwing a shell into the breech of his rifle preparatory to taking aim at the deer, when his wife reportedly spoke to him. According to officers, he half turned to answer her and his gun fired. The bullet hit Mrs. Clements just below the heart. She died instantly."

—SALT LAKE TRIBUNE SUNDAY, OCTOBER 17, 1948

Later that evening, the phone rang at my grandparents' house and Alice, who was still there, answered the call. It was an anonymous male caller.

After dinner, Mom sat at the kitchen table, clutching her heart. She was worried about Wanda. I decided to stay for a cup of tea and to help her relax. I was about ready to go home when the telephone rang. I went into the kitchen and picked up the receiver.

"Hello."

"Is this the Chaus residence?"

"Yes, it is. Who is this?"

"I'm calling to inform you that Wanda Chaus Clements

is at the Spanish Fork Morgue. She died of an accidental gun-shot wound in Spanish Fork Canyon."

"What? Who is this? And how do you know my sister?"

"I prefer to remain anonymous," said the man on the other end of the line.

"Well, then I don't believe a word you are saying," I said.

I hung up the phone and went back to the kitchen table, worried about Wanda and wondering what to tell my parents. Then, suddenly, there was a knock on the front door. I looked out the window to see who was there. It was a stranger with a notepad in his hand. I opened the door.

"Hello," he said. "I know it's late, but I'm wondering whether this is the William Chaus residence. I'm a reporter from the Salt Lake Tribune."

"Yes, I said," William is my father. I'm Alice and I'm here with my parents. Did you just call here?" I asked."

"No. I'm following up on a police report."

Once he realized this was a surprise to us, he had no choice. He informed us, gently, that the police report indicated my sister Wanda had been accidentally shot by William Clements (her husband) while they were deer hunting.

Then, the police arrived and the rest is history.

We never believed it was an accident.

—ALICE

My grandmother was in denial. She didn't believe what the police had told her. Her daughter was only 23 years old. She was certain this was a mistake even though she felt the bullet fly through her own heart earlier that night.

That night, we all went to the morgue together. I had no idea what to expect, but I was sure it was a mistake. It must be someone else, I thought. Not my daughter. Not my baby girl. How in the world could Wanda be gone?

When we finally got there and went inside, it was unreal, like being in a nightmare. It was cold and quiet—so quiet you could hear a pin drop on the cement floor. There was a man standing next to a cot where a pure white sheet was draped over a lifeless body. I wanted to crawl into the corner of the room and disappear but I stayed there, staring at the man in the white coat. Vasili and Alexandra were holding onto me, afraid I would faint. When the man lifted the sheet, I stood there, frozen, looking down at my beautiful child. She looked like she was sleeping.

Then, I fell on top of my baby as the tears poured down my face and onto her body. I couldn't imagine living my life without her. Why did I let her go deer hunting with him anyway? Especially after what she whispered in my ear? Maybe I should have gone with them. Maybe then, he would have killed me instead. He said it was an accident. How could that be? How could he accidentally shoot her in the heart?

As we were leaving, the detective handed me a bag of her clothes—the clothes she was wearing that night, including the red sweater I made her wear. When we got home, I couldn't sleep. The whole day played out over and over again in my mind. How could this have happened? Why didn't I beg her not to go? What was I thinking?

I got out of bed and made my way downstairs in the dark, carrying my daughter's clothes in the bag. Then, I placed the bag carefully in the same trunk where I had found the red sweater earlier that day—the sweater she was wearing when she was shot in the heart. The one I was sure would protect her.

—KATINA

Below is the transcript for a story that appeared in the Salt Lake Tribune the next day and Wanda's death certificate. At the bottom of the transcript, the "Other information" indicates that "Mr. Clements also had another wife at the time." However, that information (and the fact that Bill and his "other wife" had a 4-year old son) was not published in the newspaper.

TRANSCRIPTION OF TEXT

Young S.L. Matron, 23, Killed in Rifle Mishap

A young Salt Lake woman, Mrs. Wanda Chause Clements, 23, 823 South Main was accidentally shot and killed Saturday night while hunting in Diamond Fork canyon near Spanish Fork.

The bullet was fired accidental [sic] from a gun held by her husband, William P. Clements, 24, who was just a few feet away.

Investigating officers said Mrs. Clements, her husband, and a friend, Wesley Hughes, 23, also of Salt Lake City, had come through some brush onto the road when a deer was sighted to the east.

Mr. Clements began throwing a shell into the breech of his rifle preparatory to taking aim at the deer, when his wife reportedly spoke to him.

According to officers, he half turned to answer her and his gun fired. The bullet hit Mrs. Clements just below the heart. She died instantly.

Other hunters, including Lt. Charley Allred, Provo, Utah State Highway Patrol were summoned immediately. Lt. Allred sent for Sheriff Theran B. Hall, County Atty Arnold C. Roylance, both of Springville and Deputy Sheriff Ruben Christiansen, Spanish Fork, who made the investigation...The couple, who had been married about a year, have no children Mrs. Clements was born in Salt Lake City, Dec. 8, 1926, a daughter of Mr. and Mrs. William Chause. She was graduated [sic] from Granite high school in 1942. She is survived by her parents, her husband, three sisters and two brothers. Mrs. Alice Hale, Mrs. Afton Kyriopoulos, James, and George Chause, all of Salt Lake City She was married to Mr. Clements March 7, 1947 [sic] in Salt Lake City. Mrs. Clements was a member of the Greek Orthodox Church.

Detail   Salt Lake Tribune Newspaper

Date   Salt Lake Tribune Sunday, October 17, 1948

Other information   Mr. Clements also had another wife at the time

Web Address   http://newspaperarchive.com/salt-lake-tri-bune/1948-10-17

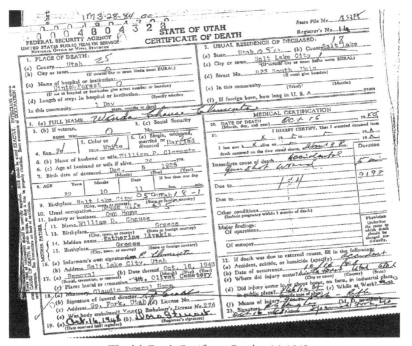

Wanda's Death Certificate, October 16, 1948

I was almost two years old when Wanda's husband (the uncle I never knew) shot her. He shot her "just below her heart." Police officers at the scene reported that a "bullet was fired accidentally from a gun held by her husband...who was just a few feet away."

Like my mother's family, I wonder, was it really an accident?

Each family member grieved Wanda's death in their own way—often unconsciously, alternating between different stages of grief—denial, depression, anger, and bargaining—despite the fact that their lives were buzzing with activity.

My grandmother began by burying Wanda's bloody clothes, along with her grief, in that basement trunk. She never opened it again.

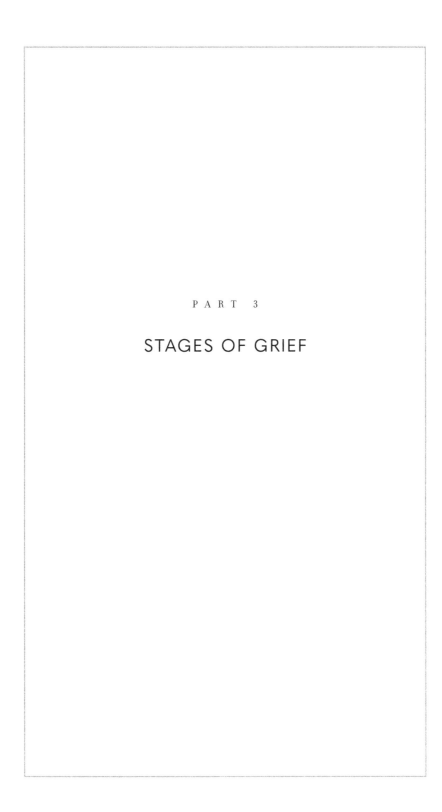

PART 3

STAGES OF GRIEF

AND THEN THERE WERE THREE

~

Alice, Afton, Anne, circa 1950

AFTER WANDA'S DEATH there were only three sisters in the family—Alice, Afton, and Anne. Anne was the oldest. Alice was the strongest. She protected her sisters and didn't let anyone push them around. Afton, my mother, was suddenly the youngest sister.

When they got together, they balanced each other out. Often, Alice (with her direct, outspoken personality) kept Anne and Afton from getting into an uncomfortable conversation.

MEMORY ETERNAL

∾

"Η μνήμη της να είναι αιώνια...May her memory be eternal."
—GREEK ORTHODOX MEMORIAL PRAYER

SHE WAS GONE again. My grandmother didn't say where she was going, yet the whole family knew she was making her five-mile trek to Mt. Olivet Cemetery to visit Wanda. She was still in the bargaining stage of grief. Grandma Chaus was a sweet, soft-spoken woman with dark hair and smiling eyes. She wore her hair pulled back in a bun most of the time. I can imagine what she may have been thinking as she walked to the cemetery.

> I always wear my best shoes and my finest black dress when I visit Wanda, even though I know my feet will swell up and my whole body will be aching by the time I get back home. The smell of Spring is in the air today. I know the bright pink crab apple blossoms are signs of a new season, but I need more time with Wanda. I'm bringing her a perfect red rose from our garden.
>
> It's been more than forty days since my sweet baby girl was swept away from us by her no good husband. I'm still praying for her. I want to know why she had to die. How could it be an accident? He shot her in the heart! And why didn't I say

anything to the police that night? Why didn't I beg her not to go deer hunting that day? Why didn't I offer to go with them? Would she have even listened to me?

Maybe I should stop at the police station on the way to the cemetery. I want to tell them what she said to me the night she died, but I don't know how to translate the words she whispered in my ear that night.

"Μπορεί να με σκοτώσει, αλλά πρέπει να πάω μαζί του!" (He may kill me, but I need to go with him!)

Wanda was always a little dramatic. I should have known better than to let her go with her husband after what she said to me that night. I'm such a fool. How could I have let it happen? Yes, she was married. But she was still a child, just 23 years old. She had so much to live for.

As I walk toward the entrance, I feel her sweet presence. The wrought iron gate is heavy. I pull it open and make my way into the heart of the cemetery. I imagine Wanda as a little girl, running beside me, guiding me to her grave. I fall to my knees right there on top of her grave and lean the single red rose on her tombstone as the tears flow like rain, watering the grass still growing on top of her.

Reaching into my purse, I find the small incense burner and the Livani (Greek incense). I light the incense and make a cross as I inhale its sweet scent.

"Η μνήμη της να είναι αιώνια." (May her memory be eternal.)

—KATINA

I am inspired by my grandmother's regular visits to Mount Olivet Cemetery. It was a long walk and she was determined to honor her daughter. I'm sure she also said a little prayer for each of her loved ones—first, for Wanda, then for William and then her other five children—Anastasia, George, Alexandra, Eftichia, and Demitri, making the sign of the cross over her heart with each prayer. I imagine she also thanked God for her three beautiful grandchildren, promising to protect them.

I envision her spending almost an hour in prayer, kneeling in front of Wanda's grave before helping herself up, holding on to Wanda's tombstone to support her weak knees and bending over to kiss the image of her daughter before saying another silent prayer —this time, for herself.

Finally, I imagine her wiping the tears away with an embroidered hanky and beginning her long journey home, remembering Wanda as a little girl. A little girl with big teeth.

> If we'd have had her teeth fixed when she was younger, maybe she would have married a nice Greek man instead of that Mormon bigamist. And what about Bill's other wife? Is she in danger, too? Maybe I should try to find her and warn her. I want to learn more about the man who killed my daughter. And I want to know why he disappeared as quickly as he appeared in our lives. If I knew where to find his other wife, I'd walk up to her and ask her why he would do a thing like that.
>
> —KATINA

Katina's heart was beginning to break. It was getting weaker every day.

~

"SHE'D GONE THROUGH hell with that guy, but she loved him," Aunt Anne said as she described her sister Wanda.

When it came to love, Anne had also gone through hell for a guy she loved. In 1947, the same year Wanda and Bill were married, Anne returned home, the prodigal daughter with a little baby boy. The baby she had kept a secret from her family for over a year. The baby her parents helped raise, pretending he was someone else's child. The baby she was determined to raise on her own at a time when most single mothers were widows.

After she moved back home, Anne went back to work at Tony's restaurant. She couldn't stop seeing the love of her life, even though she knew he was never going to leave his wife and family.

> In the meantime, dumb me, I went back to work at the restaurant in Clearfield and, yes, I kept seeing Tony secretly. I just couldn't help myself. I was still in love with the guy. Then one day, a Greek guy named Nick started coming around the house to visit. He asked me out and we ended up going out together from time to time. Then, out of the blue, Nick asked me to marry him.
>
> I thought, God, maybe this is a way out of my situation with Tony. I thought about it and talked with Mom. She was

happy about the prospect of another Greek son-in-law even though she knew I wasn't in love with him. It was my decision and I decided to marry him for the sake of my baby. He was a good man. We got married and he moved in to my parent's house.

A few short weeks later, I started getting these damn pains and I was sick every morning. I knew immediately what that meant. I was pregnant. And Nick was not the father. I didn't say anything to him or my mother, but Mama knew things. One morning, when Nick was at work and Rickie was still asleep, Mom and I were sitting at the kitchen table drinking coffee and eating scrambled eggs and toast. She was unusually quiet. As I took a bite of toast, I looked up at her. She had the saddest look on her face. She didn't say a word. She just sat there, staring at me. Then, she spoke up.

"Πανάθεμά σε (Damn you), Anne, how could you do this? I can't believe you did this again!"

"I'm sorry, Mom. I made a big mistake."

I was so ashamed of myself. I was pregnant again and Mama knew. She knew my new husband was not the baby's father.

—ANNE

Anne was pregnant again. She had been keeping it a secret again. This time she was keeping it a secret from her husband, Nick. For a few months, it was a crisis for my grandmother. Then, on October 17th, 1948, the unthinkable happened. Wanda was gone, the whole family was in a state of shock, and my aunt's 2nd pregnancy was the least of Grandma's worries. Suddenly, life was moving in slow motion. Grief is like that. It's like walking through a deep pool of thick, dark mud. The whole process is so slow and so difficult, you feel like giving up. Then, if you're lucky, something happens to get you moving.

I still remember that day as if it were yesterday. It was November 21, 1948. The whole family was still in mourning. Mom wore black every day and she couldn't stop crying. It had only been a month. I was lying in bed thinking about my baby sister. I couldn't believe she was gone. I expected her to walk in the door any minute. It was like waking up from a bad, bad dream. How could her husband have done that to her? She loved him so much.

Suddenly, I realized my bed was soaking wet. My water had broken.

"Nick, I need to get to the hospital."

I was terrified. When I got up, the water was still leaking. It was like a river flowing out of me. I said a silent prayer.

"Please, God, save my baby. I know I have been bad, but please save my baby."

Nick ran upstairs to get my mother. My father was outside milking the cows. Mom came running down the stairs and Nick called an ambulance. Dad stayed home with Rickie. Mom and Nick were by my side all the way to the hospital.

Once we were at the hospital, the doctor said he would have to deliver my baby with a C-section. Another unnatural birth. Another baby born of my bad decisions with Tony. This time, I ended up with a big scar all the way down my stomach. Thankfully, my baby was healthy. Before I left the hospital, I decided to give my second baby his real daddy's last name, but I didn't tell Nick.

Nick and I got along fairly well. I never told him it wasn't his baby. But he knew. He was a real gentleman and he wanted to get me pregnant. He tried so hard. He knew little Georgie was not his baby. We didn't talk about it because we were living with my parents. Eventually, he started staying out at night, working on the cars. He came home smelling like oil and grease and he'd jump into bed without even taking a shower. I thought. . . Oh God. I just can't stand him.

Finally, one night we were getting ready for bed and I said to him, "Nick, why don't you just leave me? Just walk out on me. I won't contest anything. Just divorce me."

He would not move. He just stuck around. I don't know why. Then, one day, out of the blue, Mom gave him some advice.

"Nick, I know you feel responsible to stay here and take care of Anne and the boys, but I think it would be best for you if you leave and start a new life. It's not working out for the two of you."

That's when he decided to leave. We never fought. We just kind of, I don't know, I guess I was still in love with Tony. After my second baby was born, I didn't go back and work for him. There was no way. Little by little, I just grew away from him. He'd caused me so much grief. And he wasn't going to marry me or anything.

I raised my two boys at my parents' farm house. I did what I could. Of course, Mom took care of them, too. I worked three days a week as a typist and a few nights a week as a cashier at another restaurant in town.

—ANNE

Once Anne decided to stop seeing her lover, she never saw him again. And her two boys never met their biological father.

THE UNIMAGINABLE

~

WITH THREE GRANDCHILDREN and work, work, work on the farm, I'm sure my grandparents held onto the rest of their children and grandchildren tightly, trying to push away the imaginable, trying to focus on a bright future of their grandchildren. Yet, the pain persisted.

My grandmother alternated between denial, depression, and bargaining. It's unimaginable to lose your 23-year old daughter. Unimaginable that she was shot in the heart. Unimaginable to be able to forgive yourself for not being there to protect her.

On November 30, 1950, she was at the old farm house where Alice and Ernie were living, helping Alice with her new baby granddaughter. Based upon my aunt's story about what happened that evening, I can imagine the scene.

"Alexandra, I'm sorry. I am so tired today. I think I will go home and rest."

"Sure, Mom. Don't worry about us. We will be fine. Thank you for stopping over to help out. When Ernie gets home, I'll come over and get the laundry I left at your house."

Worried about my mother, I waited for Ernie to come home from work and, as soon as he arrived, I walked across the field to my parents' house. It was a cool, overcast day. When I got to the back door and noticed it was wide open, I felt a chill in my bones. Mom wouldn't leave the back door open, especially on a day like today. Thankfully, Anne's two little boys were upstairs, napping. I closed the door and walked into the kitchen where I found my mother. It looked like she had fallen down trying to reach a chair to sit down, so maybe she fell asleep on the floor.

"Oh, God! It's Mama! I screamed. "What happened? Mama! Wake up! Please wake up."

Dad was outside, working. When he heard me scream, he came running inside. Mom was on the floor with her back against the wall and her legs spread out in front of her. I shook her, trying to wake her up, pleading with her. Dad was helpless. He just stood there, in shock.

"Papa, can you find a blanket? Mama is cold."

Dad found a blanket and I tried to make her comfortable. That's when I noticed foam coming out of her mouth. I was so scared. I picked up the telephone and called for an ambulance.

By the time the ambulance arrived, it was too late. Mama's heart had stopped beating. As the paramedics put my poor mother on a stretcher, I hugged Papa with all my heart.

"Well, I guess she's up there with Wanda now," he said. Tears began falling slowly from his blue eyes.

Then, we both broke down crying and hugging each other hard. My own heart started pounding, but I wasn't ready to join that party. I had a new baby girl to take care of. Papa helped me to the chair my mother couldn't reach when she fell to the floor and I sat down, clutching my heart.

—ALICE

My grandmother was only 57 years old the night she collapsed in her kitchen. At some point, the family discovered Wanda's bloody clothes in the trunk where she had buried them, along with her grief. Katina died of a "broken heart" after her heartstrings had been stretched thin. There was the death of her brother George in 1918, at least three still births, and the trauma experienced by her youngest child, Jimmy, who returned from the war in 1946, a broken boy. Then, the unthinkable happened. Her youngest daughter Wanda was shot in the heart.

> "Broken heart syndrome, also called stress-induced cardio-myopathy or takotsubo cardiomyopathy, can strike even if you're healthy...Women are more likely than men to experience the sudden, intense chest pain — the reaction to a surge of stress hormones — that can be caused by an emotionally stressful event. It could be the death of a loved one or even a divorce, breakup or physical separation, betrayal or romantic rejection."
>
> —SOURCE: AMERICAN HEART ASSOCIATION, INC.

To this day, every time I see a deer, whether it is alive or not, I react immediately with a deep reverence for life. Then I think about my Aunt Wanda and my grandmother, Katina. Ironically, I believe Wanda was trying to save a baby deer from being shot the moment before she was shot.

I am writing these stories in the spirit of forgiveness, to honor those who lived before me and to move beyond the unimaginable to a place of acceptance. Whatever happened that night, it's time to forgive.

> "O God of spirits and of all flesh, You trampled upon death and abolished the power of the devil, giving life to Your world. Give rest to the souls of Your departed servants in a place of light, in a place of green pasture, in a place of refreshment, from where pain, sorrow, and sighing have fled away. As a good and loving God, forgive every sin they have committed in word, deed, or thought, for there is no one who lives and

does not sin. You alone are without sin. Your righteousness is an everlasting righteousness, and Your word is truth."

—FROM THE TRISAGION, GREEK ORTHODOX
MEMORIAL SERVICE

IN MEMORIAM

~

AS I LOOK through the many photographs of my own mother, I see more smiles on her face before the Deer Hunting Mishap than afterward. I was about two years old at the time. I can imagine how that traumatic event altered her life overnight. And mine. Mom's grief was there whenever she squeezed my little hand, wanting to keep me safe from the horror of being shot in the heart. Then, two years later, when she lost her mother, sadness became her constant companion. Most of the time, I could see the grief in my mother's eyes, windows into her broken soul.

Mom used to tell me stories about how often I managed to knock over the floor lamp in the living room, smashing the smoky glass lampshade. Apparently, it happened more than once, so maybe it wasn't an accident.

> "Margie! You've done it again! What's the matter with you? Now, we have to go get a new lampshade before your father comes home. Hurry up, now."
>
> Frankie was in school and I was trying to clean the house. I had to grab my baby and take her with me to the lamp store to get a new lampshade before Jim came home. I had to protect my baby from a spanking.
>
> —AFTON

As I look back, I can see it all so clearly. My mom was still grieving. She wasn't ignoring me. She was keeping busy as a distraction from the pain she was feeling inside. As for me, I was just a child, determined to get her attention, and I had figured out a way to get it. Each time I knocked down the lamp, I won the prize—time with Mom. Although she told that story often, she never said a word about the Deer Hunting Mishap.

Between 1950 and 1960, four more baby girls were born in our family. Unlike my grandparents, who had six children and welcomed a new baby just about every year, it took my parents 17 years to give birth to six children. My father worked long hours at the service station and Mom was always busy with the babies. She dressed us up like little dolls and took very good care of us, physically. We were her perfect little darlings. All her life, her goal was to protect her children from life's unimaginable traumas. Meanwhile, her own life was full of anger, paranoia, and depression. Unable to trust others, even those who were closest to her, she was never able to heal from the wounds of her past.

Me, Mom, Frankie, Kathryn, and Dad, circa 1952

Whenever I saw a photograph of Wanda, I'd ask my mother to tell me about her sister, hoping to hear some stories about this beautiful sister who was no longer with us. My mother's responses were always about her death, not about her life.

"Her husband shot her in the heart during a deer hunting trip."

"It wasn't an accident."

"He was already married to another woman when he married my sister."

That was that. End of conversation. I didn't even think about asking a follow-up question because it seemed to be too much for my mother to handle.

Still, if it wasn't an accident, why did Wanda's husband shoot her? And, if it was an accident, how did he manage to accidentally shoot her just below the heart? We will never know the answer to these questions and the only way to move beyond our inherited grief is to come to a place of forgiveness.

Every year, on Memorial Day, we went to Mt. Olivet cemetery to visit Wanda, my grandmother Katina, and my grandfather William. The three of them were buried side by side, Wanda between her parents. Hers was a place of honor in our family. The beautiful, oval-shaped image of my aunt affixed to her tombstone is fixed in my memory.

BEWARE OF GREEKS BEARING GIFTS

~

George and Elaine Chaus, July 29, 1951

WHEN UNCLE GEORGE returned from the war, he fell in love with a young Greek woman, but Grandpa had already found a wife for him. Elaine was the daughter of one of his friends, so George followed in the Greek tradition of arranged marriages. He and Elaine were married a year after Grandma died.

After George and Elaine were married, Dad gave them a piece
of property next to the farm so he could build a house there.

—ANNE

He was the oldest son in the family and I'm sure Grandpa wanted
him to take over the family farm. I can imagine him presenting this
"gift" to Uncle George.

"George, Congratulations to you and Elaine! I have a piece of
property right here. Next door to the farm. Now that you're
married, I am giving you and Elaine that piece of property as
a wedding gift."

—WILLIAM (MY GRANDFATHER)

Based upon my brief conversation with Uncle George, I can't imagine him wanting to take over the family farm. Also, according to Aunt
Anne, he kept the property for a few years before he and Elaine bought
a house on the "East Bench." He didn't want to upset his father, but
eventually he sold the property next to the farm.

Of course, Grandpa found out. Selling the "gift" his father had
given him did not go over well. Grandpa was a stubborn man. My
grandfather never forgave his son for selling that piece of land. By this
time, Grandpa was working at Union Pacific Railroad again because he
couldn't manage the farm on his own. He was angry at George, yet he
never said a word.

Seven years later, when Grandpa died, Pandora's Box opened up
and his anger spilled out in black and white. When his will was discovered, the family learned that he had given his entire estate—the farm, the
farmhouses, and all the furnishings—to his daughters and his youngest
son, James, who was still a patient at the Veteran's Hospital in Salt Lake
City. His oldest son, George, was not even mentioned in his will.

After Mom died, Dad stayed with us for a few months and he told me he had already given George a piece of land next to the farm. I didn't realize he was talking about his will until after he was gone. He never went into the details, but when his will was read, it was like George wasn't a member of the family. He wasn't even in the picture. If only he'd have told George he wasn't going to leave him anything because he had already given him a piece of land, maybe things would have turned out differently, but he didn't say anything to George. It didn't come up until we saw it in the daggoned will. So, what the heck?

We used to get together with our kids from time to time. Eventually, our families grew apart and that was the end of it.

You know, I blame the guy who put the damn thing together. Dad's will should have said something like, "I divide this property equally between my children, except for my oldest son George because I already gave him a piece of property next to the farm."

It could have been so simple. Instead, it was like my brother didn't exist.

—ANNE

Although it was a Greek tradition for sons to inherit the parents' property and daughters to inherit furniture and household items, my grandfather decided to get even with his oldest son by leaving him out of his will entirely. Looking back, I realize that my mother and her sisters didn't even think to offer George a fair share of the estate. They simply accepted their father's ill will, sprinkling rock salt on their brother's wounded ego.

No wonder I hardly knew my uncle and his family. Year after year, the valley between the families grew as deep and as wide as the Grand Canyon. They were never there for birthday gatherings, Christmas parties, or Easter celebrations—all big events in our family. Likewise, they didn't invite us to their special events either. Over time, the wounds of the past seemed to deepen and I knew Uncle George and his family like I knew other members of the Greek community—from a distance.

There was an unspoken agreement between my uncle and the rest of the family and I was always uncomfortable with that agreement. When we were young, my siblings and I vowed we would never let anything like that come between us, yet there were moments when I was judgmental about how my sister was managing both my parents' estates. Something deep within me took over emotionally. It came from an unexamined place in my own experience.

As Socrates said, "ὁ … ἀνεξέταστος βίος οὐ βιωτὸς ἀνθρώπῳ" (The unexamined life is not worth living). Eventually, I was able to examine the source of my reaction, share it openly with my sister, and forgive myself. This is a reminder for future generations of our family: Your children and your children's children are the beneficiaries of more than your property. They are also beneficiaries of your reactions to each other.

LIFE IS GOOD

~

AUNT ANNE DANCED through life, living each day as a new experience. She was a loyal employee and a loving mother of two young boys who, despite the challenges she faced as a single mom, always looked at the bright side of every situation. When she met a man who professed his love for her and his desire to take care of her and her boys, she saw it as a way to give her sons a better life, a more normal life for a woman with two young children. It was 1955, five years after my grandmother died of a broken heart.

Roy Swartz and Aunt Anne at Our Home, October 20, 1955

When I met Roy, I thought he'd give me a good life. I wasn't in love with him, but he kept sending me these cute little notes, "Beautiful lady" and "You're so sweet." And he was good to the boys, too. He worked for a dairy company in American Fork, about 30 miles south of the city. Roy was a smart business man and, golly, I'd be making a mistake if I didn't marry him. We got along pretty well and I thought, "Life is good with this man."

We got married at city hall and my sister Afton hosted a little reception for the family at her house. The whole family was happy for me now that I was going to settle down with a man who wanted to take care of me and the boys. Pretty soon, I started dreaming about us having our own home with a yard where the boys could play.

"Roy, why don't we get a house? I don't see any sense in paying all this money in rent," I said to him.

"Okay, Anne. Why don't you go out and look for a house and see what you can find?"

So, my neighbor and I went out looking for houses. It didn't take long to find my dream house. I fell in love with the darn thing. It was in a nice location, about halfway between my two sisters' homes. It had a beautiful, fenced yard with a white picket fence. The sign out front read, "For Sale by Owner."

"My Godfrey," I said to my friend, "This is my house!"

I took Roy to see the place and he could tell I was in love with it. Even though it was a longer drive to work for him, he wanted me to be happy. So, we moved in and made regular payments to the owners until we finally paid them $4,000 for the down payment. Then, we assumed their mortgage, which was neat. Sadly, though, by the time we finished paying the down payment, Roy decided he didn't want the damn house.

"Anne, I think we should move to American Fork, closer to my work."

Oh my God, I thought to myself, I'm working. I can afford to make the payments myself.

"No, I cannot do that. I just can't. I love this house."

Eventually, Roy decided he didn't want to stay here with us anymore. He wanted to live in American Fork. On weekends, I'd cook a roast with potatoes and carrots and take the kids there so we could be together as a family. Then one day, Rick got into something at his place and Roy got so angry, he pulled at his ear until it bled.

Boy, I thought, this is it. There's no way I'm coming back up here. No way.

—ANNE

After that day, my aunt didn't go back to American Fork to visit her husband on weekends. Roy visited her and the kids in Salt Lake City from time to time. During their marital separation, she became close to a man who had just lost his 39-year old wife. It was 1958 and the two of them were members of their own lonely hearts' club. In their efforts to console each other, they got a little too close.

I couldn't believe what I had done. I was still married to Roy even though we were living separately and, stupid me, I ended up sleeping with my good friend. One day, Roy came to visit and I told what had happened. I told him I had gotten myself in trouble. It was the truth. I was pregnant.

"Well, it's definitely not mine," said Roy.

"I realize that. I didn't say it was yours. I'm just telling you that's what happened."

I guess I wasn't very smart because if I'd have been smart, the other guy would have married me and I'd have had everything. He was an engineer, a well-established gentleman and a friend of our family. After I told him about all my problems, he wasn't sure whether it was even his baby. I knew it was his baby because he was the only man I had been with while Roy and I were living separately. I guess he just didn't want to get involved in my life. Anyway, he ended up marrying another woman and, after the baby was born, Roy and I ended up getting divorced. This time, I gave my baby Roy's last name, even though he wasn't the father.

That was one of the biggest mistakes I have made in my life. The other big mistake was not telling my son about his real father until he was teenager. His father called me a couple of times over the years and I thought he was going to come over and see us. He never did. He just couldn't do it. The last time he called, our son was 12 years old. Later, I learned he had killed himself. I don't even remember who told me but I cried like crazy when I heard the news.

Oh, I don't know. What a mess. What a mess I've made of my life.

—ANNE

My aunt lived in denial after the Deer Hunting Mishap. She didn't want to think about all the bad things that happened around her and to her, so she just tried to forget about it all and enjoy life's pleasures. She took life a day at a time and went out dancing as often as possible.

Her affairs were a big family secret when I was growing up. After she told me her stories, I wondered whether her parents' fear that she was pregnant out of wedlock had become a self-fulfilling prophecy. She proved them right three times. Then, in her early 70s, she met Athol, a widower. They met on the dance floor.

"I fell in love twice—once in my twenties and again in my seventies," she told me. Tony was my one true love until the day I met Athol at the

Senior Center. Of course, we met on the dance floor. After we started dating, I told him my whole life story and he still wanted to marry me. That was a big thing to me."

Although Anne was hesitant to marry Athol because of her personal history with love and marriage, she finally agreed and they were married in 1992. She was 74 years old when she married her second true love. It was a short, happy marriage.

Two years later, Athol died in his sleep, peacefully.

THE CASE OF THE MISSING STAMP COLLECTION

~

SOMETIME AFTER OUR family moved into a larger house until the day she died, my mother had her own conspiracy theory. She was convinced Anne's oldest son had stolen my brother's stamp collection from the cellar. Mom was both judge and jury in the Case of the Missing Stamp Collection. She was stuck somewhere in the past. Was she reacting to my aunt's affair with a married man by accusing her son of being a bad boy?

Anne and Afton on New Year's Eve in Atlanta, Georgia, 1998

Mom seemed to be unable to have an open, honest relationship with Anne. The missing stamps in my brother's collection kept getting in the way. She kept her distance, avoiding her sister and often "forgetting" to return her phone calls. She was usually judgmental behind her sister's back. One day, when the two sisters were together having coffee at Mom's kitchen table, it all came tumbling out. My mother finally confronted her sister years after her initial accusations against Anne's oldest son.

> "Your son is a thief! He stole Frank's stamp collection and I know he stole it! I have proof. I overheard him saying anybody could take anything out of that cellar. That's how I know he did it!"
>
> —AFTON

This conversation happened long after my brother's stamp collection went missing. Both of their sons were married and had two children of their own. Still, my mother was unable to let go of Frank's missing boyhood stamp collection.

> You know, I believe we need to forgive and forget. I know I need to forget what she said to me. What really hurts me the most is that my sister did not come to me right off the bat and tell me that my son stole her son's stamp collection! If she would have done that years ago, I might have been able to do something about it. I didn't know all the stuff she was thinking until much later.
>
> —ANNE

I am beginning to believe my mother's anger came from a much deeper place within—a place she was never able to explore.

"Afton, why are you telling me this now?" I asked her. "What can I do now? What is the point of that?"

"Well," she said, "I didn't want to tell you earlier because I didn't want to hurt you."

"So, what do you think you are doing now?" I asked her. "You didn't want to hurt me so long ago, but you're telling me now. Fifteen years later, you're telling me this dumb story. That's what really hurts."

"Well, I thought you might see if you could find anything at Rick's house. Frank is struggling right now and he could use the money."

"God, my son is married! I wouldn't know what to look for and I wouldn't do that anyway." I said to her.

So much for all that. I wish it was different. But I guess it's not going to be. Even though I'm not as close to some members of my family as others, I can't imagine not wanting to spend time with them. My sister has hurt me in so many ways. Although there were some little things earlier in our lives, things were okay between us until she accused my son of stealing from her.

—ANNE

The missing stamp collection came up more than once, directly and indirectly, even after my brother said he didn't give a damn about the stamps. The truth is, my mother was never able to let go of her anger.

Grief presents itself in unpredictable ways. My mother's need to protect her son's stamp collection was a reaction to something deeper in her heart. Perhaps the loss of her innocent young sister, Wanda.

~

MY MOTHER'S FAMILY had a history of keeping secrets and telling lies, but the truth eventually emerges as the stories unfold.

I always thought I knew my Aunt Alice well. She was often perceived by others as aggressive, yet I believed her strong personality was her saving grace. When my grandparents tried to pull Alice out of school in 9th grade as they did with Anne, she resisted. She went directly to the principal and asked for his help in convincing her parents she needed to finish high school—even if she was a girl. Her persistence paved the way for Afton and Wanda, who also finished high school.

Alice didn't go to church every Sunday, even though she was a devout Orthodox Christian. She kept a little altar of icons and candles on her nightstand and I imagined her on her knees, saying her prayers every night before she got into bed.

She spent long hours filling orders for the most popular records on vinyl, typing juke box record labels, and managing a small team at a local record distributing company. She would bark at anyone who didn't follow through on their part of the job, a true taskmaster. She knew the executive salesmen for big record labels like Capital, Decca, and Columbia on a first name basis. My favorite Christmas gifts as a teenager were the hit demo records (45s) from Aunt Alice.

After I graduated from college, I struggled to find a job as an English major with a minor in Philosophy. Aunt Alice recommended me to

John Billinis, the owner of Billinis Distributing, the music record distributing company where she worked. He was a Greek immigrant. After my interview, he offered me a job as a Receptionist/Bookkeeper at $350 a month. I tried to convince him I was worth more. After all, I had a college degree. I'm afraid I wasn't blessed with Aunt Alice's strong personality. I needed a job, so I decided to accept the job offer. Eventually, I won him over by gently editing his broken English business letters and within six months, he rewarded me with a generous salary increase.

From time to time, Alice and I went out to lunch together at the Busy Bee on State Street where we feasted on large, greasy, fried Pastrami sandwiches. Working together, we became more than family. We became friends. Alice inspired my love of all kinds of music, from Classical to Country. I never doubted her wisdom and honesty.

We began a tradition of going to church services together during Holy Week. Usually we went to church on Good Friday, one of my favorite Holy Week services. During the service, an icon of Jesus is laid in a tomb (Epitafios) decorated with bright red and white carnations. In a somber reenactment of Jesus Christ's crucifixion, Bible passages are read, hymns are sung, and the priest leads a procession outside, around the church. The whole congregation follows the priest and the Epitafios carried by deacons and altar boys, each member carrying a lighted candle.

Sometime during the season, we would get together and make Greek pastries—Baklava, Kourabiethes, and Koulourakia. I asked my aunt for the recipes and she typed them for me on recipe cards using the same typewriter she used to type song labels for the jukeboxes. These recipe cards have traveled with me through all of my many moves.

Sweet!

BAKLAWA

1	lb	Butter
1	lb	Walnuts (Chopped)
1	lb	Almonds (Chopped Fine)
1	lb	Filo
3/4	Cup	Gran Sugar
2	TBS	Powdered Cinnamon
		Cloves (whole)
½		Tsp Allspice, nutmeg, mace, Ground Cloves (opt)

Mix together nuts, sugar & spices
Pastry brush Butter Bottom pan
12x18'..Lay 5 sheets filo buttered
seperately-Add thin layer nut
mixture-repeat with one filo sheet
(buttered) then nut mixture. Re-
peat till all nut mixture is used
Add 5 sheets (buttered) on top.
(do not butter top sheet) With
serrated knife cut pastry into
one inch squares or diamonds
but do not cut thru the bottom
layer. Add whole clove in each
square. Bake °375-10 Min. °350
10 Min. °300-30 Min. 200° 10 Min.
Remove from oven cover with syrup
while hot--FINISH CUTTING BOTTOM
LAYER.

OVER

SYRUP

4	CUPS SUGAR
3	Cups Water
2	TBS Lemon Juice--Plus Rind
2	Cinnamon Sticks

Boil Together 10-15 Min.
Cool--pour over pastry.

ALLOWING PASTRY TO STAND 24 hrs.
HELPS BLEND FLAVORS.

KOULOURAKIA

1	lb butter (left to soften)
1	Doz. Eggs
4	Cups sugar
1	Cup Half & Half Cream
3	Heaping TBS Baking Powder
1	Tbs TBS Vanilla
1	Tsp Baking Soda
½	Cup Brandy
5	lbs Flour (less one cup)
	Orange or Lemon Juice opt.
	Sesame Seeds

Beat eggs until frothy--CREAM
Butter until light--Add eggs,
sugar, cream, brandy, vanilla tp
butter. Blend together well
slowly add flour & all powdered
ingredients to right consistancy.
Roll & Shape. Bake °425 for
15 Min.
Beat 2 Eggs & 1 TBS milk in
saucer. Brush on cookies.

SESAME SEEDS OPT.

KOURABIETHES

1	LB Butter (Melted)
2	Egg Yolks
½	Cup Powdered Sugar
1	TBS Vanilla
½	Tsp Baking Powder
½	Cup Ground Almonds
4	Cups Flour
2	TBS Brandy
1	Orange (juice & Rind) Opt.
	CLOVES

Beat melted butter with beater
one half hour. (light & fluffy)
Add Sugar & Egg yolks--blend.
Add all other ingredients except
flour. Mix Well. Lastly blend
in flour. Knead well. Roll
out dough into round or diamond
shaped balls. Add whole clove
to each cookie. Bake °350 about
20 Min. Roll in powdered
sugar until well coated while
cookies are still hot.

Alice worked hard and she played hard. Every year, on New Year's Day, she hosted an open house. Food and drink flowed in abundance and music played on the stereo. Holiday tunes, Billboard hits, Classical favorites, and Greek music. Eventually a chain would form and everyone would practice Greek dancing. My Godfather, Harry, often the lead dancer, always twirled around as he led the Syrtaki (Zorba) with a white cloth napkin in his hand.

One year, I sat alone in the living room while everyone else was downstairs celebrating the new year. The lights were low and Alice's modern aluminum Christmas tree, complete with an electric color wheel, glowed in the dark, lighting up the room as it slowly changed from red to blue to green. It was the 1950s and my aunt was on the leading edge of holiday decorating. Hers was so different from our annual holiday tree—a perfectly shaped tree finally purchased after an hour-long search through the cold outdoor tree lot. Our tree was always perfect (Mom approved) with multicolored lights, glass ornaments, and icicles carefully placed on each branch.

My husband and I carried on the tradition of decorating live Christmas trees for years. Then, one day when I was living alone in Fairfax Virginia, I saw a cute little retro aluminum tree with tiny white Christmas lights at Michael's and I thought about my Aunt Alice. I took it home, opened it up, and decorated it with retro glass ornaments in her memory.

When my aunt finally retired, she bought a single level condo in South Salt Lake and settled in to her new retirement home. For as long as I can remember, she was a heavy smoker and she enjoyed the night life—drinking and socializing. Perhaps it was her way of rebelling against Mormon doctrine of abstinence from alcohol, tobacco, and caffeine. In retirement, she looked forward to spending time with her grandchildren after a long career as a working mom. Then one day, three years after she retired, she suffered a severe heart attack. She made it to the hospital where her heart failed again. This time, her weakened heart didn't make it. She was just 68 years old. Her heart was beating in a delicate balance. This, too, runs in the family.

I knew Alice had a secret—I knew she and Ernie had eloped and were secretly married in Nevada back in 1942. Ernie returned from WWII in 1945 and their first child, Kathy, was born in 1946, a year before I was born. Kathy was named after our grandmother, Katina. Alice and Ernie had two more children together but their marriage ended in divorce. Later, she married a man who was a heavy drinker with two young girls who needed a lot of attention. It was a stressful relationship that didn't last long.

As it turns out, there's more to her story.

One day, as I was working on my memoir, I got a phone call from my cousin Kathy. It was likely no coincidence that I was in the process of writing the story about how her parents fell in love at the Farmer's Market. As kids, Kathy and I played together all the time. We had sleep overs at each other's homes and visited each other's schools. But as we grew up and got married, our paths began to diverge. We rarely saw each other after I moved to Minnesota.

Kathy and I chatted about our children and grandchildren. Then, she paused. I waited for her to continue and she did.

"Margie, my sisters and I decided our families should all get DNA tests to learn more about our family's history," she said.

Then, she paused again.

"When the DNA results came back, I found out Ernie is not my biological father. At first, I was sure the test was wrong so I sent away for a DNA test from a different company. It's true. Ernie was not my biological father."

My cousin was heartbroken and angry at her mother who had kept this secret all her life.

I was speechless. This unexpected news popped up like an instant message in my head.

What?

"Oh my....I can't believe this, Kathy. I am working on a memoir about the Chaus family and I just finished writing a story about how your parents met and fell in love at the Farmer's Market in Salt Lake City."

"Wow. That's interesting," said Kathy. "Well, I'm still processing it all. Ernie is the only father I knew all my life. I wonder whether he knew and I wonder why my mother never told me. I was never really close to her, but now I'm angrier at her than ever! This all happened so long ago. At my age, it doesn't make any sense to go back and try to figure it all out. Well, maybe for medical reasons it would be good to know. Anyway, my sister is determined to discover who my biological father is."

This devastating discovery took my cousin back to the day she was born to try to make sense of it all. How does anyone begin to piece together the details of a lifetime that suddenly boils down to a string of molecules?

Alice worked in the music business. She met a lot of male executives from big record companies. As I listened to Kathy, I was in a state of shock. I no longer knew what to make of Alice's little bedside altar. Did she pray to God for forgiveness? Of course, God knows the truth. She couldn't keep any secrets from God. Did she have an affair? Was it a one-night stand? Was she raped? Anything is possible.

The truth is, Alice, who was never quiet, had quietly betrayed her own daughter. In fact, she had betrayed us all.

I thought I knew my aunt. I believed she always spoke the truth, even if it hurt. I thought she may have been the one member of her generation who was able to move beyond the trauma of the Deer Hunting Mishap. Now I'm not sure about anything. Now I realize I must find my own path through our family's traumatic past to heal the grief I had unconsciously inherited. Now I feel like I'm listening to Paul Harvey on the radio, waiting to hear "The Rest of the Story." Eventually, the truth reveals itself.

PART 4

MY GENERATION

Frankie and Margie, circa 1950

MY   GUARDIAN   ANGEL

∾

AS I TELL these stories, I am untangling a web of secrets, lies, and unimaginable events from the past. Aunt Wanda is a silent presence, always
there in the background. She is my personal Guardian Angel.

Growing up, my brother and I were a childhood "couple" of sorts.
We were buddies. Frankie and Margie. Life was good. We were the first
two children in the family and we had come to rely on each other. By
1950, Mom had lost her little sister to a shot in the heart and now her
mother was gone, the victim of a "broken heart." She was a distracted
parent.

One day, while she was preparing dinner in the kitchen, my brother
called me downstairs. I believe I was three years old and he was seven.

"Margie," he called from the bottom of the stairs. "Come here. I
want to show you something."

I was sure it was a new game, so I made my way down the stairs and
followed his voice.

"I'm in here, Margie."

He was in the small bathroom around the corner. I slowly walked
toward the bathroom. The door was open and he was sitting on the
toilet with his clothes on.

"Are we playing hide and seek?" I asked.

My brother didn't say a word as he pulled me toward him and gently
pulled down my panties. Then he started touching me. When I realized

this was not a game, my immediate reaction was to pull up my panties and run. Even as a child, I was a survivor.

"Momma," I cried, running in my white stride rite walking shoes on the black and white linoleum squares, around the corner, and up the stairs.

I'm not sure what I said to her once I got upstairs, but I remember being alone in my bedroom afterwards, looking up at the framed picture of a guardian angel—a beautiful, magical, blonde angel in a flowing robe helping two little children walk across a broken bridge. Whenever I was afraid, Mom would remind me that my guardian angel was always there, protecting me.

The image of that guardian angel still looms large in my memory. For the first time in my life, I felt like I was one of those little children walking across a raging river and I knew my guardian angel was there with me.

Guardian Angel by Lindberg Heilige Schutzenegel, German artist, circa 1900

Mom obviously had no idea how to handle that situation. Grandma had recently died of a broken heart and she was pregnant with her third child. She went downstairs and talked with my brother. Then, she came back upstairs and into my room. She gave me a big hug. I don't remember her saying a word after that day, yet her silence spoke volumes. It instructed me to file away what happened to a place deep in the recesses of my memory and to forget it ever happened.

Master of famous quotes, my mother used to say, "Out of sight, out of mind."

SANTA CLAUS AND ELVIS PRESLEY

~

AS A CHILD, I was a firm believer in the Tooth Fairy, the Easter Bunny, and Santa. They always pulled through for me. Like most kids, I had every reason to believe in these magical beings. In fact, even at seven, I was a big believer in Santa. I never imagined I'd see him in person at Nibley Park Elementary, my grade school, yet there he was up on the stage during a holiday production on the day before Christmas vacation.

"Ho Ho Ho...Merry Christmas to you all!" said Santa, as he jumped up onto the big stage in the auditorium. I was thrilled to see him up on the stage! He invited us all to come up and get a candy cane and a small gift from his bag, so we formed a long line around the room to greet him personally. When we got back into the classroom, my best friend Natalie looked over at me.

"Your dad sure makes a great Santa!" she said, popping my bubble of joy.

"What are you talking about?"

"Yeah," said Suzanne. "Santa was your dad for sure. His hands were dark and greasy and they smelled like gasoline."

"No. You are both wrong! That was Santa!" I insisted.

"Well, there is a real Santa," said Natalie, "but that guy was your dad."

I was shattered. And embarrassed. Of course, I couldn't prove them wrong. I hadn't even noticed his hands—or his voice. According to my observant friends, the smell of gasoline, so familiar to me, was proof of Santa's secret identity. I finally accepted the fact that it was my father under that Santa suit, proud to have been given the gift of a dad who was Santa for all the kids at my school.

I'm sure my mother, future PTA president, was involved in the Christmas program.

My faith was shattered, but not broken. I was able to hang on to my belief in the real Santa for at least another year until the day my cousin Kathy told me the truth and burst my bubble for good. By that time, I was ready to face reality.

Another memorable event at Nibley Park Elementary took place when I was in sixth grade, ready to graduate from grade school. Everyone was in the auditorium again, watching some very talented kids perform. There were violinists, pianists, and vocalists. When it was time for the big finale, I looked up and there he was. Elvis. AKA Frankie K, my 15-year old brother! Not only did Frank have a great voice, he looked a lot like the young Elvis Presley. In fact, he practiced singing Elvis songs at home all the time. But when I saw him standing up there on stage, I was amazed. With his long sideburns and his hair all greased up, it could have been Elvis himself! He was wearing skinny blue jeans rolled up at the ankles and a silver studded cowboy shirt. Just like Elvis. To make it even more authentic, he topped it all off with a black leather jacket and hand-painted, blue suede shoes. He was swinging his hips and singing, "You ain't nothing but a Hound Dog" in front of the whole school. All the girls started screaming and cheering.

It was like we were watching Elvis on the Ed Sullivan show.

My brother, who was an Eagle Scout and spoke Greek fluently, was also an Elvis impersonator.

I'm sure Mom was involved in the decision to feature Elvis in the school talent show that day. She knew how to make things happen.

Years later, after he retired from the Air Force where he served our country as an intelligence officer, he returned to the stage again. Throughout his career, Frank was able to keep deep secrets for the Air Force, but his true passion was being an undercover Elvis Presley. In fact, during Bill Clinton's tenure as President of the United States, Hilary Clinton invited my brother to perform at the White House on Elvis' birthday. He reminded us often that he was happy to have lived longer than Elvis, the King of Rock n' Roll even though he had some heart problems of his own.

At the age of 61, Frank underwent his second open heart surgery to replace a Bovine heart valve with an artificial heart valve. The night before his surgery, he called to let me know. I was driving, so I pulled over to answer my cell phone. He was anxious.

"Margie," he said. "I just wanted to call and let you know that I'm having heart surgery tomorrow at Walter Reed Hospital. Hopefully, the new artificial valve will be better than this one."

"Oh my, Frank. I am so glad you called to let me know. I'll be praying for you."

"Thank you, Margie. I love you."

The long, complex surgery was successful. However, my brother's life was cut short shortly afterwards during recovery. According to the doctors, he experienced an allergic reaction to the Heparin, which is commonly used after surgery to prevent blood clots.

Frank was a big presence in my life. He was my brother and best friend for much of my life and I was finally able to forgive him for his antics in the basement. Now I remember all the good times we had growing up and I will forever miss his contagious laughter and his famous Elvis impersonations.

"Frank E. Kaye" Performing in Maryland, Wisconsin, and
Washington D.C.,Courtesy of Christine Kyriopoulos

HOUND DOG

When I was just a child,
a sixth grader
at Nibley Park Elementary
my friends and I watched my brother, Frankie,
young Elvis, swing on stage
singing, heart and soul,
"You ain't nothing but a hound dog,
cryin' all the time..."

We loved Elvis
and I loved watching my big brother
on that stage.

Little did I know
that my brother, Frankie,
would return to the stage
after a forty-year hiatus
as Elvis II, "frank e. kay,"
an older Elvis,
still singing, heart and soul,
"Love me tender, love tender true,
all my dreams fulfilled."

Every time I watch frank e. kaye
on stage
I see young Elvis, my brother,
in 1958, singing,
"You Ain't Nothin' but a Hound Dog,"
and swinging his hips.

~

Me, Mary, Frank, Kathy, Debbie, Mom at Carlsbad Caverns, 1958

IN THIS PHOTOGRAPH, we are visiting Carlsbad Caverns in New Mexico during one of our summer road trips. It is 1958 and my father had been working long hours at Nibley Park Service, his service station across the street from the Nibley Park Golf Course. At that time, our family of seven lived in a red brick bungalow about a half a mile away from my father's service station and a few miles away from the farm where my mother grew up.

My father's favorite way to get away from it all was to take the family on summer road trips. We drove all over the western states—Idaho, Nevada, Arizona, Wyoming, Montana, and California—exploring the National Parks and visiting our parents' relatives and friends. Although my father kept the family on a tight budget, he always splurged on summer vacations, birthday parties, and holidays. Often, we stayed at Best Western motels along the way and ate at local restaurants near our motel, so Mom got a vacation from cooking as well!

Dad had a passion for photography and always took photos of these important family events. He spent hours in his little darkroom in the basement next to the washer and dryer. I can still remember the smell of chemicals in the basement where he carefully developed all the black and white prints that became lasting memories.

❁

"Like silt deposited on the cogs of a finely tuned machine after the seawater of a tsunami recedes, our experiences, and those of our forebears, are never gone, even if they have been forgotten. They become a part of us, a molecular residue holding fast to our genetic scaffolding. The DNA remains the same, but psychological and behavioral tendencies are inherited."

—DAN HURLEY, "GRANDMA'S EXPERIENCES LEAVE A MARK ON YOUR GENES" *DISCOVER MAGAZINE*, JUNE 25, 2015

I CRINGE EVERY time I see a dead deer on the side of the road or in the bed of a truck during deer hunting season. Could this be a reminder of the Deer Hunting Mishap, even though I was too young to remember it?

I do remember the sad refrain, "It wasn't an accident," a phrase which had become an integral part of my existence. It appeared from time to time, like a Greek chorus, reminding me of the generational drama playing itself out on the stage of my life.

My reaction to a slain deer likely influenced my taste buds as well. I have always hated deer meat. After each successful deer hunting expedition, my relatives proudly prepared Stifatho, a Greek stew made with large chunks of meat and whole onions in a rich tomato sauce.

"Margie, this is Beef Stifatho. Just taste it," my Godmother pleaded with me.

I was sure Aunt Helen would never lie to me, so I tasted it. Immediately, I spit it out. It was definitely venison; not beef. I knew better. Perhaps my reaction was based upon the Deer Hunting Mishap. Or perhaps it was it just because venison tasted differently. I will never know. Yet to this day, I can't bring myself to eat venison.

Each year, on Memorial Day, our family drove to Mt. Olivet Cemetery with bouquets of colorful, fresh carnations, roses, hyacinths, and daffodils for Aunt Wanda, my grandmother Katina, and my grandfather William. The three of them are buried side-by-side, Wanda between Grandma and Grandpa. She was honored and remembered on the tombstone as the beautiful young woman, an image as fixed on her tombstone as it is in my memory.

At some point, during one of our annual Memorial Day pilgrimages to the cemetery, we noticed the image on my aunt's headstone had been vandalized. It was as though someone had used a hammer to shatter her face. My mother took one look at the tombstone and couldn't help herself. She broke down, crying uncontrollably. She tried to hold back her tears as she cleaned up the area and placed a bouquet of red mums in the metal vase in front of Wanda's tombstone.

"It wasn't an accident," she whispered.

She didn't need to say it. I knew intuitively what she was thinking. She was wondering whether Wanda's husband or someone in his family was responsible for destroying my aunt's image. After all, he shot my aunt in the heart.

'Wasn't it enough to shoot her in the heart?' I thought. 'Who would do a thing like that?'

Wanda's tombstone was not the only one vandalized, but this was personal. I have always wondered who was responsible for destroying hers. To this day, I hope it was simply a random act of violence.

I also wonder why my mother's family didn't try to restore her tombstone. Maybe they believed it would happen again if they restored it. Maybe they did restore it and it did happen again. Maybe it was too painful a reminder of the trauma to find the original image.

Over the years, I held on to that image of Wanda in my memory. Whenever I visited the cemetery, in my mind, I saw the face of my beautiful aunt, not the vandalized image.

We will never know whether the Deer Hunting Mishap was, in fact, an accident. Wanda is gone but not forgotten. Her memory is eternal.

REVERENCE FOR LIFE

∿

"REVERENCE FOR LIFE" has been my mantra for as long as I can remember. Perhaps it began the night of the Deer Hunting Mishap, even though I was just a baby. Albert Schweitzer's words have stuck with me throughout my life.

> "Reverence for Life affords me my fundamental principle of morality, namely, that good consists in maintaining, assisting, and enhancing life and that to destroy, to harm, or to hinder life is evil..."
>
> —MAURICE BASSETT, *REVERENCE FOR LIFE:*
> *THE WORDS OF ALBERT SCHWEITZER*

In 1963, I was a Sophomore at South High School. Our high school was as close as you could get to a melting pot community in Utah. November 22 started out as a day like any other. When the bell rang for the next class, my friends and I strolled down the hall, chatting as we made our way to the next class when an announcement came over the loud speaker.

"This is an important message from the office of the President of the United States." Full stop. "President Kennedy has been shot in Dallas, Texas."

What? I couldn't believe it.

We stopped walking and stood there, looking at each other without saying a word. We were in shock, immobilized, in the middle of the hallway trying to absorb what we had just heard. Then, we heard it again. The same announcement.

"This is an important message from the office of the President of the United States. President Kennedy has been shot in Dallas, Texas."

Next came the chaos.

Each of us reacts to the unimaginable in our own way. Shock, denial, anger, sadness, fear. My reaction was to remain immobilized. I couldn't believe what I had just heard and I wasn't able to move forward. I just stood there. I was in a state of shock.

How could it be? How could President Kennedy have been shot?

The rest of that day at school is a blur in my memory.

What I do remember is that when I finally got home, Mom was sitting on the sofa bed in the family room. Her eyes were glued to the small TV screen across the room. As I came down the landing from the kitchen into the family room, she looked up at me with tears in her eyes. She, too, was in shock. The whole event played over and over again on every channel. Images of the day's event flashed on the screen.

Jackie Kennedy, wearing a pink wool Chanel suit, threw herself over her husband's body in an act of pure grief. The bodyguards rushed in to protect the president. Meanwhile, Walter Cronkite announced the news of the day in his characteristic, matter-of-fact tone. His face, however, revealed his sadness.

"From Dallas Texas, President Kennedy died at 12:30 PM today."

Images of Lee Harvey Oswald flashed on the screen. Then, Mrs. Jaqueline Kennedy arrived at Andrews Air Force Base escorted by Robert F. Kennedy, her brother-in-law. She stood next to Vice President Johnson as he was sworn in to become the 36th President of the United States. The First Lady was still wearing her blood-spattered, pink suit. Several people had asked her to change her suit. Jackie refused.

"Oh, no ... I want them to see what they have done to Jack," she said.

Suddenly, on live TV, my mother and I watched Jack Ruby shoot the suspect, Lee Harvey Oswald, as he was being escorted to jail by police officers.

"Oh my God," my mother cried out.

After that day, I tried to avoid the news but it was everywhere—in the newspapers, on TV, and in every conversation. President Kennedy's assassination consumed our collective attention for weeks. My mother, grieving over her favorite President's death, watched TV all day long, sitting quietly with a blank stare on her face.

Did the assassination of her favorite President, take her back to the day her sister was shot in the heart?

My own reaction to gun violence mirrors my mother's reaction in the aftermath of President Kennedy's assassination. In my college days, I marched for peace in Salt Lake City with a group of liberal students— proud to be among them. I wore psychedelic printed tops, bell bottom jeans, and a single daisy in my long, dark hair. I had my ears pierced for my 18th birthday and bought a guitar with hard-earned money from my part-time job at Auerbach's, my mother's favorite local department store in Salt Lake City.

Although being a hippie in Utah was not the same as being a hippie in Berkeley, California, I was proud to be a rebel with a cause. I sang along with Joan Baez and the Beatles and I silently chanted, "Make love, not war." Tears streamed down my face whenever I saw the stark images of war— a young girl running naked, toward the camera, a North Vietnamese soldier with a gun pointed at his head—a daily barrage of pain spread out on the front pages of the Salt Lake Tribune. It didn't matter where I was—in a classroom, in the Crimson Commons (student lounge), or alone in my bedroom—I felt like I had been shot in the heart and I wanted to know why.

Why were we killing all those innocent people?

War is hell. And guns, the weapons of war, now control our country's collective fear and loathing. Every time a gunman (it's usually a man) kills innocent people as they go about their ordinary day-to-day activities, many of whom are children, I think about my aunt Wanda. In her memory, I will march forever in an effort to end gun violence in our country. It is a never-ending story.

SUNDAY MORNINGS

~

Kathy, Jami, Debbie, Mary, and me in Salt Lake City, Utah, 1963

EACH SUNDAY MORNING, we all dressed up for church. By the time Mom had finished dressing Jami, the youngest, she was exhausted. Dad usually drove us to church. Mom never had time to get herself ready in time for church.

~

IN THE SUMMER of 1960, the summer before my first year at Irving Junior High School, our family moved into a large, white, two-story house with blue trim and a white picket fence in the back yard.—the house my father had proudly purchased without my mother's approval.

The Christensen family lived next door. They were devout Mormons with five children. Susan Isabelle Christensen, a short, dark-haired girl with freckles and a large heart, soon became my best friend. We were both 14. Susan's sense of humor was one of her best qualities. Maybe that's because she was born on April Fool's Day.

Susan used to brag about how she was named after her grand-mother, Isabelle. Susan Isabelle Christensen. Deep down, though, she never wanted to end up like "Granny," who spent her days sitting in her rocking chair calling out to anyone who happened to be around when-ever she needed something. Susan seized every opportunity to tease Granny, who demanded too much of everyone's time and attention, especially her mother's.

One day, Susan and I were making saltwater taffy in the kitchen when Granny called out for help. Initially, Susan pretended not to hear her pleas. Then, as Granny's voice got louder, Susan snickered for a few minutes.

"Susan! I need to go to the bathroom!"

Finally, Susan popped her head into her grandmother's room. "Hi, Granny! Did you call me?" she asked cheerfully.

I loved observing Susan's antics. She always knew how to surprise and entertain me, even when she teased me for being too slow on our bike rides. Susan was also full of grand ideas. One summer in the early 1960s, she suggested we go swimming at the Ramada Inn on State Street, pretending to be guests. We wore our swimsuits under our summer clothes, put two towels in a beach bag, and rode our bikes over to the Ramada Inn. Then, we walked in as though we were guests and used the bathroom where we stripped down to our swimsuits, put our clothes in our beach bag, and snuck out to the pool.

Once we were poolside, Susan would loudly announce, "Hi! We just came down from our room to go for a swim!"

One hot summer day, we invited Susan's older sister, Jo Marie, and her 10-year old brother, Frankie, to join us on our trip to the pool. Frankie loved swimming! Everyone in Susan's family loved swimming— and they were all better than I was. I was afraid of the deep water after a bad experience as a child in swimming class when I had forgotten my nose plugs. That day, I dove into the deep end, inhaled water into my nose, and ended up gasping for breath as I struggled to come up for air. I thought I was going to drown.

We were all enjoying our adventure at the pool that afternoon. Frankie loved to dive into the deep end and swim laps, splashing as he swam. He was so happy that day. Then, he dove into the deep end and, suddenly, the splashing stopped. Susan called out to Jo Marie, who was lying on a towel, tanning by the side of the pool.

"Jo Marie! It's Frankie! He didn't come up after he dove into the pool!"

Jo Marie jumped up and dove into the pool, pulling Frankie out. Instinctively, she lay him down and began mouth-to-mouth resuscitation.

The image of my best friend's brother, a bright, wiry little boy, lying limp and lifeless on the hot cement with his big sister hunched over him, breathing life into him, one deep breath after another, is stuck in my memory. Susan and I stood there, shaking, for what seemed like forever.

Finally, Frankie started breathing on his own and I was sure I had witnessed a miracle. After that day, our motel swimming adventures were over. Susan and I made a silent pact never to sneak into a swimming pool again even though we never talked about it. I often wondered whether we had been punished and I was ashamed of myself for betraying my own nature. I was born on February 12th, the same day as Honest Abe, Abraham Lincoln. And I had lied.

After that, we only went swimming at Fairmont Park, a public pool in the Sugarhouse neighborhood, one of the oldest neighborhoods in Salt Lake City. Most of our friends lived in that neighborhood. Sugarhouse was between the west side of town (where mostly middle class, blue collar families lived) and the east side of town (where mostly white collar upper middle-class families lived). We swam at the public pool almost every day in the summer. Sometimes we rode our bikes and sometimes Susan's mom came with us. I was surprised to see her Temple garments under her modest swimsuit. It was the first time I had ever seen Mormon underwear.

Two years later, Frankie was swimming at Fairmont Park with his friends. Once again, he disappeared in the deep end. This time, his sister wasn't there to save him. We weren't at the pool that day and Jo Marie wasn't there either. Frankie ended up in a coma at the hospital. I couldn't bear to see him lying in that hospital bed, hooked up to plastic tubes and a breathing machine. After two weeks, his parents decided to take him off life support.

I couldn't believe it. Susan's brother Frankie was gone. How could this happen to a such a great swimmer?

I later learned that he was diagnosed with a congenital heart condition. "Jumping into a cool pool after being in the hot sun shocked his little heart and lungs," said the doctors.

Susan wasn't about to let her young brother's death interfere with her bizarre jokes. One of her favorites was a joke about a woman who answered the door and saw a young delivery boy with a telegram in his hand:

> "Well, don't just stand there, young man. Sing it to me!"
>
> The delivery boy protested, saying he couldn't sing the telegram. But the woman insisted.
>
> "Well, if you can't sing it to me, I won't accept the telegram."
>
> "Okay...," he said, quietly. "If you insist."
>
> The boy hesitated for a moment before he sang softly, "Dear Mrs. Jones...I regret to inform you...that...your son is dead."

Most of us had a hard time laughing at that one, even though it was pretty funny. Susan, on the other hand, told that joke over and over. Even as a 15-year old, she was able to accept death as just another part of life.

Susan and I were like twins though I was a lot taller. We both had dark brown (almost black) hair and we both wore white bobby socks, brown and tan saddle shoes, and plaid wool pleated skirts. On game days, we wore our royal blue pep club dresses. In the winter, we wore navy blue pea coats.

Sue Christensen   Marjorie Kyriopoulos

From "The Southerner," South High School Yearbook, 1965

We took sewing classes together and Susan was not only a better swimmer, she was a better seamstress too.

I remember spending hours in her basement bedroom chatting about our young lives. Though neither of us liked to gossip about our friends, we almost always talked about the boys we liked. I also remember parties with our friends when we lip-synched to our favorite Beatles songs in her living room, flapping our hair around as we pretended to be playing guitars. "I Wanna Hold Your Hand," "She Loves You, Yeah Yeah Yeah" and more.

When we were sophomores in high school, a certain Mormon Bishop told my friends that I was "loose" with guys and insisted that they stop spending time with me, even though all of them knew I had never even kissed a boy. In fact, one of my friends actually tried to convince me to make out with some boys at her house one night. I refused. "Goody Two Shoes," they called me. That year, I learned an important lesson about the meaning of true friendship. Two of my friends rejected the Bishop's advice and remained friends with me. One of them was Susan. It was a silent, powerful statement. She was a true friend.

By the time I was a junior, I got a part-time job as a waitress in the Tea Room, a restaurant in the basement of Auerbach's, a classic downtown department store, working Saturdays, summers, and holidays. Although my job took me away from lazy Saturdays hanging out with Susan, I enjoyed earning a little money. One day, Bessie, who was a manager in the Marking Room, paid for her lunch and asked me whether I would be interested in working for her.

"It's a better paying job, Margie." Bessie was a member of my church. I saw her every Sunday.

Soon, I would be going to college and I would need more spending money. I decided to check it out. A few days later, Bessie took me on a tour of the area. The different machines were humming so I didn't hear much. But I saw a lot. About ten older women stood on the cement floor, each performing their own tasks in an assembly line manner using price tagging machines, staple gun machines, clothing steamers, and more. There were racks full of fancy dresses, wool coats, and shiny formals.

Bessie did offer more pay, but it meant working in a dark, windowless basement and standing for long hours on cement floors—isolated from the customers and fancy departments. It was a tough decision. Eventually, I accepted her offer. My job was to put price tags on underwear using a staple-gun machine, inserting the elastic band on each pair of panties into the machine. Yes, I did put a staple through my fingernail a few times. My favorite diversion was when Bessie asked me to go upstairs and mark down items that were going on sale. Using a purple pen, I drew a line through the original price on the tag and wrote the sale price above it. I loved that part of my job because sometimes I got a great deal on new outfit for myself!

After we graduated from South High School, Susan and I were both accepted at the University of Utah. She was studying to be a social worker and I wanted to be an elementary school teacher. I joined the Kappa Alpha Theta Sorority and my circle of friends grew to include non-Mormons. Susan eventually joined Alpha Chi Omega. We didn't see each other as often, yet no matter long it had been, it was as though time stood still. Whenever Susan saw me smoking a cigarette in the "Crimson Commons," the student lounge, she'd walk up to me, extinguish my cigarette in the ashtray, smile, and walk away.

I let her do it every time.

Fast forward to November 1968. Jim Bradley and I were married on November 24th. We didn't wait to graduate from college. We found a small, cheap apartment near the University of Utah where we were both actively engaged in the Anti-Vietnam War Movement. When I heard Susan was dating a guy named Randy, who was also active in the local Anti-Vietnam War Movement, it was the best news I'd heard in a long time. Randy looked a little like Kevin Costner. He was handsome and had a contagious smile. He was also a good Mormon. He and Susan were the perfect couple!

A week before she graduated from the University of Utah, Susan and Randy came to visit us. It was a good sign that marriage was in their future. We had a fun time together and I was excited about being best couple friends forever. Within weeks, Susan was about to receive a degree in Social Work.

The day after Susan graduated, I was listening to the Beatles on the radio when I got a call from my mother. She was crying and I could barely understand her.

"What's the matter, mom?"

"It's Susan," she said.

"What about Susan? I saw her a few days ago."

"Margie, I can't believe it. I just talked with Freda. Susan was swimming at the Deseret Gym after her graduation ceremony... and...just like Frankie...her heart and lungs stopped."

"What???? No! That cannot be!" I screamed.

"She's gone, Margie."

I was in shock. All I could hear was the Beatles singing in the background, "Let it Be, Let it Be..." a song I will forever associate with my best friend, Susan Isabelle Christensen. I immediately started in with my mental judgments. Didn't the doctors test everyone in the family for congenital heart problems? How could this happen? She was a strong swimmer! Then, the Beatles interrupted my thoughts. "Let it Be...Let it Be..."

In that moment, I created my own silent memorial service for my best friend. She was 23 years old on the day she died—the same age as my Aunt Wanda on the day of the Deer Hunting Mishap. To this day, whenever I hear that song, I honor the memory of my best friend, Susan Isabelle Christensen.

QUE SERÁ, SERÁ

～

GROWING UP IN a large Greek family was like going to the circus. You never knew what was going to happen from one minute to the next. In fact, whenever I asked my mother a question about my own uncertain future, she broke into a song, "Que Será, Será, whatever will be, will be..." singing the first stanza of the song made famous by Doris Day.

One cool, October evening when I was still in high school, I was getting ready to go to my friend's house. It was getting chilly out, so I asked my mother if I could go down to the cellar and get a sweater out of the trunk where she stored our winter clothes.

"No, Margie. You can't!"

I was surprised by her immediate and decisive reaction.

"Why not?" I asked in my raised, teenage voice. "It's getting cold and I want to wear a sweater to the party."

"Absolutely not!" My mother was adamant. "Your grandmother took a sweater out of a trunk for my sister one night and guess what happened? She died that night!"

I looked at my mother, speechless.

What could I say? I knew better than to argue with her. Instead, I thought about my mother's strong response. Maybe it's just a superstition. It doesn't mean something will happen to me. Her reaction was clearly her final answer, so I left home without a sweater, thinking about how I could test my theory.

A few days later, I made a plan. I was determined to prove my mother's fear was an irrational superstition. My plan was to sneak downstairs alone and get a sweater out of the trunk. Did I want to free myself from carrying around that trauma for the rest of my own life?

While everyone was watching TV in the back of the house, I quietly slipped out the front door and walked around the side of the house. I stepped quietly down the cold cement stairs, nervous, but determined, and opened up the creaky wooden door into the dark, damp cellar.

Stubborn. Just like my mother.

I pulled on the string to turn on the light, a bare bulb overhead, and snuck inside. Making my way through all the old furniture and boxes, I found the trunk and opened it up. Quickly, I pulled out my favorite pink mohair sweater and made my way to the cellar door. Then, I pulled the string again to turn off the light, closed the wooden door, and snuck up the cellar stairs. I re-entered the house quietly and hid my sweater in the coat closet.

The next morning, on my way out the door to wait for my ride to school, I reached into the coat closet and quietly stuffed my sweater into my gym bag. Though I was always pretty quiet, on this particular day, I was keeping a big secret. I hadn't said a word to anyone about my plan to solve the mystery of whether opening a trunk at night could cause a death in the family. It was a serious experiment.

Once I got to school, I went directly to my locker, opened my gym bag, and pulled the sleeves of my pink cardigan sweater over my white, cotton, oxford shirt. I was wearing a pastel plaid skirt, so it was a perfect match. I wore my favorite pink sweater all day long, wondering whether anything bad would happen that day.

I'm happy to report that my experiment was a success. Nothing bad happened to anyone in our family that day, or that night. I was proud of myself, but I knew better than to tell my mother about the results of my science project. It was my secret. To share it would open up the trauma of the Deer Hunting Mishap, a subject which never came up unless we were at the cemetery or looking at an old family photograph. I wonder now whether my mother's reaction to my simple request came from a deep-seated fear that was woven into her heartstrings—a legacy as real as any genetic marker in her DNA.

To this day, I wish I'd have known my Aunt Wanda as a person. What was she like? Was she as fun-loving as she looks in her photographs? Did she and Mom play together when they were kids? Were they close to each other?

Over the years, Mom's favorite way to communicate with us was through famous quotes. It was her way of preaching without saying a word. Sometimes she would recite one as a reminder to heed a piece of sage advice. They could be found all over the house. Her favorites were featured in the laundry room just outside the main bathroom where she kept a gallery of memorable quotes clipped from magazines and newspapers and pinned up on a bulletin board above the laundry hamper. Whenever I had to go to the bathroom, I would reflect on one of her favorite quotes on my way to the "throne."

"It is never too late to be what you might have been."

—MARY ANN EVANS

"You can fool all the people some of the time: you can even fool some of the people all the time; but you can't fool all of the people all the time."

—ABRAHAM LINCOLN

A woman of few words, my mother was blessed with a gift for sketching. She was an artist. When we were young, she often doodled at the breakfast table. One morning in 1968, I was upstairs getting ready for my first class of the day at the University of Utah. Mom climbed up the narrow flight of stairs and paused in the doorway of Jami and

Debbie's bedroom. She seemed to be thinking, 'Why must I wake them? They are so peaceful.' She woke them anyway, gently nudging each of them in a way only mothers know how to do. Then she went back downstairs and opened a can of Minute Maid frozen orange juice, mixed it up with three cans of water in a pitcher, and set the table with two glasses of juice, two bowls, and two spoons for Jami's favorite breakfast, Corn Flakes, and Debbie's favorite, Rice Krispies.

Debbie, the "little lady," wandered into the kitchen first, stretching her arms toward the ceiling.

"G'morning, Mom."

Jami, the "little pixie," made her entrance to a new day more slowly. The three of them carried on a short conversation. Debbie and Jami jabbered on about whatever happened to come to mind. The topic of discussion that day was my upcoming wedding. The girls had a million questions, but Mom interrupted them, pointing at the clock on the wall reciting a couple of her favorite quotes.

"School starts in a half an hour! You need to get going! Hurry up now and finish your breakfast. Think about all those children who are starving in Africa!"

Quickly, my little sisters swallowed a couple of spoons full of cereal and finished their orange juice. Then they ran upstairs and rushed around, getting their school supplies together.

"Don't forget to brush your teeth!" my mother called out to them from the bottom of the stairs. As soon as they came bouncing down the stairs, she rushed them both into the bathroom to part and comb their hair. Then, she scooted them to the front door, kissed them each goodbye, and stood there, silently watching them walk to the bus stop.

She locked the front door and went back into the kitchen where she poured Jami's soggy Corn Flakes into Debbie's bowl of Rice Krispies which were no longer snapping, crackling, or popping, and sat down to finish off what I used to call "the breakfast of mothers."

In a few weeks, I would be getting married. It was a short engagement and I was ready to start a new life as a good wife and the best mom ever. That was my dream.

THE ROAD LESS TRAVELED

~

LIKE MY MOTHER, I sometimes wonder, what if I had taken a different path? What if I had decided to take the road less traveled? What if I had taken the road my mother was unable to take?

My journey to adulthood began in 1968. I was at a turning point in my life. Things were getting serious with Jim Bradley. One night, he arrived to pick me up for a date and asked to talk with my dad. I was surprised and so was Dad. Jim was a tall, handsome 22-year old. He was my knight in shining armor. That night, he was wearing a freshly pressed, white dress shirt, tails hanging over his faded blue jeans. Very cool. He reminded me of Marlon Brando in "On the Waterfront." I thought he looked absolutely dashing. He walked right into the kitchen with his characteristic, bouncy gait and popped the question.

"Mr. Kyriopoulos, I am in love with Margie. Could I have your permission to marry her?" Jim asked, smiling and confident.

Dad looked at him and thought about what he had just been asked. Then he said exactly what he was thinking.

"Well, Jim, here's my advice to you. Get yourself a real job so you can afford buy your own shirt instead of wearing your dad's shirt. You know, he's bigger and taller than you are. Anyway, come back and ask me again when you are able to support my daughter."

Jim was deflated, but we were in love and determined to be together.

The sexual tension was building between us, but I was determined to be a virgin on my wedding night. A few weeks later, I got a call from my cousin Teresa about a summer job in New York City. Perfect solution! At 21, I was excited to travel somewhere during the summer between my Junior and Senior years at the University of Utah. I didn't even think to ask her more about the job. I trusted my cousin.

During finals week, I got another call from Teresa. The job was no longer available. I was not happy to hear the news, but I could hear my mother's voice in the back of my mind.

"Que Será, Será…"

Then, one day, during a break between finals, Sue, a graduate student in the English Department, came up to me.

"Uh. Hi…I heard you talking about your plans to get away for the summer…just wondering… are you interested in going to San Francisco? I'm planning to drive there next week and I will also need a roommate for the summer. You're welcome to join me," she said.

"Wow! Thank you. I'd love to hear more about it!"

We had a few conversations and I talked with my parents. When I told them Sue was older and reminded them that Uncle George, my father's brother, lived in San Mateo, they agreed to let me go.

"Well," said my mom. "California is much closer than New York City!"

Once the decision was made, it seemed to happen overnight. I was going to see the world before settling down in Salt Lake City.

A week later, we drove off in Sue's car and I waved goodbye to my parents, who were standing on the front porch.

Everything was going smoothly until Sue's car broke down in Winnemucca, Nevada. Somehow, we made it to an auto repair shop and, luckily, there was a motel nearby.

"The least expensive room is one double bed," said the motel manager.

Sue looked over at me.

"Hmm. Well, I have four sisters, so I'm used to sleeping with them in one bed," I said.

"Okay," she said to the motel manager. "We'll take the room with one double bed."

It had been a long day, so we went to bed early that night.

In the middle of the night, I awoke, startled. My new friend had turned over in the bed and begun to caress me in a way I had only been touched by my mother. It was somewhere between a mother's and a lover's touch.

What? Was I dreaming?

I got up and went to the bathroom where I thought about it for a few minutes. I grabbed two cushions from the sofa, threw them down on the floor, and made a bed for myself.

The next morning, my traveling partner looked at me, surprised.

"What's wrong?" she asked.

"You know what's wrong," I said emphatically.

She acted like she didn't know what I was talking about. Was she dreaming? Did she mistake me for her boyfriend?

I had no idea whether she had a boyfriend or not. But I did have a boyfriend. I was still a virgin at 21 even though I had been making out with boys since high school. Confused and unsure of how to handle the situation, I convinced myself she was asleep, dreaming she was with someone else, and hoped the car would be ready so we could get back on the road.

Sue went next door for breakfast and I took my time getting showered and ready for the day, trying to forget the whole incident. When I got to the restaurant, she was chatting with some young women at the diner, exchanging phone numbers and having an animated conversation with them. Hmmm. Interesting. After breakfast, we walked over to the auto repair shop to get an update on the car repairs, hoping we could check out of the motel and get back on the road. No such luck. The parts were being shipped to the repair shop and hadn't arrived yet. We were stuck at the motel for another night.

For dinner, we decided to go to the bar across the street. There were some guys who worked for Pabst Blue Ribbon sitting at the bar. They bought us a few beers and I flirted with them all night long. I wanted to make sure Sue could see that I was attracted to men. She was flirting with them, too. Whew!

We staggered across the street and back to our motel room. I decided to give it another try and climbed into my side of the bed. Sure enough, once again, I awoke when she began petting my shoulder. It was a touch so gentle, yet so uncomfortable. This time, I knew it was real. Once again, I got up and made myself a bed of sofa cushions on the floor. And, once again, the next morning, she wanted to know why.

"Don't you know why? Really?" I asked.

"No. I have no idea why you are sleeping on the floor."

Again, I was speechless. Too young to know how to handle the situation, I thought about my options. I could call my parents and ask them to come and get me, but I was an adult, almost a college graduate. It was time for me to grow up and experience the adult world. Still, I had no words to explain why I ended up sleeping on the floor two nights in a row. I didn't know how to explain that she had violated my boundaries. I was so naive.

Once we were on the road again, I felt like a frightened kitten, hiding from the alpha cat in control of the car and my life. When we got closer to San Francisco, she called her friends in Berkley. They invited us to stay with them until we found work and a place to stay in San Francisco. When we got to their house, I grew an inch taller in my awareness. The two women were definitely a couple. They were gracious and kind. I respected their openness and appreciated their hospitality, wondering whether they thought we were also a couple. At this point in my life, I did not know anyone who was (at least openly) homosexual. I never imagined the need to explain my own heterosexuality and I had no idea how to do so.

As we chatted with her friends, my mind was working overtime. Clearly, this was not going to work out for me. I tried to figure out a way to separate myself from an uncomfortable situation unsure how I would break the news to her. I asked if I could use the telephone to call my uncle. Uncle George answered the phone and I quietly described my situation. He invited me to stay with his family until I found a job in the city. Huge sigh of relief. Avoiding the inevitable, I graciously lied to my new friend and her old friends.

"My uncle insists that I stay with his family in San Mateo until I find a job in the city," I said. "He can pick me up here tomorrow and take me there. Thank you so much for your offer to stay here, but I haven't seen my family in San Mateo for a very long time."

Uncle George picked me up the next day and I agreed to stay in touch with Sue. Thank goodness it was a weekend! Uncle George was an executive at a tobacco company headquartered in San Mateo and he traveled a lot. He, Mary Lou (his second wife), and my cousin Carolyn graciously welcomed me into their home. I spent a few days comfortably recovering from my journey and I shared my story of the trip with them. I read the San Francisco Chronicle classifieds religiously, looking for a job to get me through the summer. We called my parents to let them know the situation. They thanked Uncle George profusely.

Uncle George took me to the train station every morning on his way to work so I could look for jobs in the city and I went to the movies with my cousin Carolyn in the evening. Finally, I was hired as a proofreader for a newsprint tabloid on Market Street. That job lasted one day. It didn't pay well and I couldn't imagine sitting in an uncomfortable chair reading tiny newsprint all summer, especially since my commute from San Mateo to San Francisco wasn't supposed to be a permanent solution.

As it turns out, there **are** angels in America. Just as I was ready to give up and consider going back home, I ran into a friend of a friend of mine from Utah. She invited me to stay with her and her two roommates in the city until I found a job and another place to stay. She recommended that I find an employment agency.

"It's free to use an agency here. The employer pays for them to find employees."

Although she welcomed me with open arms, I knew I needed to find my own place to live. Her roommates were cordial, but not as generous with their friendship. I told my new temporary roommates the story of my journey to San Francisco.

Within a week, I found a job through an agency. I lied to get the job. I did not tell the agency I was planning to return to Utah in the fall. I was hired to work at Traveler's Insurance Company, typing claim details, mostly numbers, all day long. It wasn't a great job, but it was better than proofreading tiny newsprint. And, I loved my new manager. He called me Roxanne because he said I looked like a Roxanne. He was a fun-loving, kind, Irish man.

Inevitably, I got a call from Sue. She wanted to meet for lunch and talk about finding a place to live. She, too, had found a job in the city. It was time for me to break the news to her even though I had no idea whether I could afford a new place to stay on my own. We met at a restaurant on Fisherman's Wharf. The smell of the sea and fresh shrimp filled the air. I knew it was time to let her know I was not going to live with her.

"It's not going to work out for us to live together," I said.

Again, Sue was amazed. I couldn't believe it.

"What do you mean it won't work out?" She screamed at me.

"You know what I mean." I said softly, still afraid to say what I was thinking ("It won't work for us to live together because I am heterosexual.")

I was afraid to speak up for myself and say, simply, "I'm not attracted to women." I was afraid she would deny everything again, so I just sat there, watching her lose control as she yelled at me and attacked me out loud for leaving her stranded. Eventually, she got up from the table and left in a huff.

I breathed a huge sense of relief, even though I still didn't have a place to live.

A few days later, my three new roommates invited me to join them for dinner and a comedy show in the city. In a simple twist of fate, we ran into Vicki, another expat from Utah living in San Francisco. She joined us for dinner and the show. As it turned out, she was looking for a roommate. She lived in a studio apartment on the corner of Leavenworth and California. It was a perfect location for me to catch the cable car to and from my office at Traveler's. We spent some time getting to know each other and she, too, listened patiently to the story of my trip from Salt Lake City to San Francisco. We agreed to meet at her apartment that weekend. We would have to share a Murphy bed, but she said not to worry because she, too, was attracted to men. Whew! I was happy to have found a new roommate and friend.

I left home that summer believing I was wise and worldly. What I learned was that I was ignorant and naïve—just a small town girl trying out her independence. I grew up, awkwardly, overnight, struggling to become an adult in the big city. Like Dorothy in the Wizard of Oz, I was no longer in Utah. Sometime after I returned home, I learned that my penultimate roommate in San Francisco was also a lesbian. She didn't say a word as I shared all the details of my nights on the road in Winnemucca. She simply listened with her heart, gave me advice about how to find a job, and offered me a space in her apartment. When I realized how she must have felt as I told her my story, I felt like a fool.

Although I didn't give up on my dream of seeing the world, I wish I had been more direct with Sue, the woman who challenged me to be true to myself.

I met Donald the day he and his friend came to visit Vicki. From that day on, the four of us got together regularly. When Vicki and I decided to move to a larger apartment, the guys helped us make the move. Our new apartment at 1360 Clay Street had a lovely red awning at the front entrance of the building. The apartment building was nestled between the Grace Cathedral and Chinatown. I felt like Mary Tyler Moore in San Francisco, living a life of luxury on a shoestring. As a foursome, we often got together on the balcony outside our new apartment and watched the sunset. It was the best happy hour in town. I loved being with my new friends and I loved my summer job at Traveler's Insurance.

Donald was a simple young man. He usually wore a tan t-shirt and brown corduroy Levi's. He had dark hair and a soft smile. He was quiet and calm. Maybe because he smoked pot every day. He worked at Travis Air Force Base, so I was surprised he went to work under the influence on a daily basis. Donald knew I was almost engaged, but I sometimes noticed him watching me as we drank wine and hung out on the balcony.

One day, he came to the apartment by himself.

"Margie," he said, "I need to tell you something. I don't care about your boyfriend in Utah. I care about you."

I was shocked. Amazed. And confused. After that day, Donald and I spent Saturdays driving up Highway 1, along the Marin County coastal highway, in his white VW Beetle with a blanket and a picnic lunch we'd purchased at a little deli in Mill Valley. We drove along miles of green, rolling hills where cows grazed and children sold lemonade along the side of the road. It was the perfect way to spend Saturdays together.

One night, after our country drive, we were alone in the apartment and Donald convinced me to smoke a joint with him. I had never tried marijuana. I was nervous, but I decided to give it a try. We smoked and chatted and relaxed as the Doors played in the background, "Come on baby, light my fire..."

Before I realized what had happened, we were lying next to each other on a blanket in the living room, kissing and hugging. From that moment on, there was no turning back. I had fallen in love.

The next day, Sunday, I was beside myself. I wandered into City

Lights Bookstore looking for books about pregnancy tests. What if I were pregnant? I knew better than to get myself in that situation. Smoking pot was amazing—and dangerous. I wanted to stay in San Francisco instead of going back to Utah, but I had no idea how to make that happen.

First, I called my mother. Surely she would understand my dilemma. She always wanted to move to California.

"Hi, Mom."

"Margie! What a surprise to hear from you. Are you okay? This call must cost a fortune."

"I'm doing well, Mom. I called because I wanted to talk with you about my trip back to Utah. I'm thinking about changing my plans and staying here in San Francisco. I can live here for a year, become a resident, and finish school here tuition-free."

"What? Are you kidding me? That is ridiculous. You are about to graduate from the University of Utah. Why on earth would you do that?" she asked.

I was silent. It was never productive to argue with my mother. She knew why I wanted to stay in San Francisco. She knew I had a boyfriend. She became Demeter, determined to rescue me from my big city, hippie boyfriend. As usual, she was right. It was a boy. Like Persephone, I had tasted the sweet fruit of the pomegranate.

"Margie," she said loudly, " You need to come home and finish school in Utah. You can move back to California after you graduate. You'll be able to get a better job with your college degree."

Her argument made sense. Especially, since I was a team leader responsible for the new student orientation program. Although she had never been on an airplane in her life, Mom flew to San Francisco, determined to bring me back home to Salt Lake City. She met Donald and we took her on a whirlwind tour of the city, cable cars, Chinatown, Fisherman's Wharf, and more. She was enjoying the tour even though she was on a mission—to escort me back home.

My mother had lived most of her life in Salt Lake City, except for her brief stay in San Diego. Although her Greek name meant happiness, she was not a happy woman. She often talked about her dream of moving to California, yet here she was, dragging me away from my desire. Finally, I agreed to return to Utah. It was the sensible thing to do. The day we boarded the airplane was bittersweet. Donald couldn't bring himself to see me off. Maybe he was at work. All I remember is crying as I waved goodbye to Vicki and boarded the airplane with my mother.

In my heart, I was singing along with Peter, Paul, and Mary, "I'm Leavin' on a Jet Plane..."

Once I returned to Utah, I moved into a dorm room for Orientation week. A few days later, Donald called. He was on his way to Salt Lake City.

"I want to marry you, Margie," he said

"Donald, I have good news! I got my period. I'm not pregnant."

"Oh, I'm sorry. I was hoping you were pregnant, so it's not good news for me," he said. "I'm still coming to Salt Lake City. I want to spend the rest of my life with you."

"Okay...I can't wait for you to meet the rest of my family."

Well, my dad had already decided he was a bad influence on me, a hippie from San Francisco who had brainwashed me. I knew what he would say. He and Mom kept talking about how I had changed.

"You're a different person, Margie," said my mother.

True. I **had** changed. I was no longer the obedient young woman whose purpose in life was to please her parents. Being back home was like going back in time. My travels on the road and in San Francisco had transformed me into an adult and there was no turning back.

The next day, I told Jim about Donald and his marriage proposal. His response was to ask me out on a date.

"I'd like to take you out to dinner tomorrow night. How about your favorite restaurant, The Cinegrill?"

"Okay," I said, softly. It was the least I could do. I had vowed not to have sex until my wedding night. But here I was. In the middle of a big dilemma.

Jim picked me up for dinner the next evening wearing a suit and tie. He rarely dressed up like that. My father was impressed. He had reserved a quiet corner table at my favorite Italian restaurant. Almost as soon as we sat down, he took a small package out of his pocket and opened it. In his hand, he held a beautiful, antique-looking, golden wedding ring. The wedding band and engagement ring fit together like pieces of a puzzle. The engagement ring featured antique roses and tiny diamonds with a larger, shiny diamond in the center and the thin, winding wedding band fit perfectly into the engagement ring—a symbol of the union between two people joined together in matrimony.

"Will you marry me?" He asked. "I know the diamond isn't very big. I also know you like flowers more than gemstones."

He knew me well. I was a flower child. What a surprise! I had no idea he was going to propose to me that night. To top it off, he had already talked with my dad, who was on his side now.

"Margie," he said. "If you're pregnant, I still want to marry you."

What? How did he know I was worried about being pregnant? Was that the change my parents saw, too?

Donald would be arriving soon, expecting to marry me and take me back to California with him. Now, Jim had asked me to marry him. My friend had warned me that he didn't stay with one girlfriend for long before he found a new one. Yet, here he was, asking me to marry him.

"I need some time to think about all of this," I said.

"Okay. Just remember, I'm serious. I love you. This ring will be waiting for you if you decide your answer is yes."

Donald arrived a few days later with only the clothes on his back. Someone had broken into his VW Beetle parked in front of his apartment the night before he left town. They stole everything. We had some long conversations about Greek weddings and clearly his idea of marriage was less about the wedding and more about the vows. He was right. It is more about the vows.

"Donald, I need some time to think about all of this." I said. Then, I told him about Jim's proposal.

A few days later, we said our goodbyes and I promised to let him know my decision. It was a difficult time for me. I was confused and disoriented. I tried to focus on my upcoming role as a new student orientation leader for freshmen entering the University of Utah, but I wasn't sure whether I could fully commit to this responsibility in my state of mind.

During student orientation, I spent a week at the dorm, trying to function as though everything was normal. My peers saw right through me. Nights were sleepless and days were difficult. I spent the entire week analyzing my situation. Most of my high school friends got married almost immediately after graduating from high school, so I was definitely old enough to get married. Donald was a heavy pot smoker and there wasn't enough information about the effects of marijuana on children of users.

Jim wanted to marry me even if I were pregnant, which I wasn't. That was a game changer. He didn't even know the details, yet he loved me enough to accept me even if I was carrying Donald's baby.

A few weeks later, I called Jim.

"Hi, Jim," I said. "I'm calling to see if you still want to marry me?" He didn't hesitate.

"Of course. I want to marry you, Margie," he said. "I love you."

"Well, I have made my decision. It's Yes! I am honored to be your wife."

I ended up writing a "Dear Donald" letter and sending it off to him. Since that day, I have not heard from him.

Jim and I decided on a very short engagement. It was August and we were married the following November. It was a "Big Fat Greek Wedding" celebration.

Marjorie Lin and Edwin James Bradley, November 24, 1968

I felt like such an adult at 21. Still, I wonder, what if I had taken the road less traveled, dropped out of school a year before graduation, and stayed in California?

THE BEGINNING OF THE END

~

BY 1960, MY parents had been married for 25 years, yet signs of discontent were in the air. The first sign appeared the day my dad came home and announced that he had some big news. His voice was full of excitement.

"I've found us a bigger house!" he said.

Mom stood there and looked at him. She was silent. She couldn't believe her husband had gone out and bought a house without consulting her. Mom was a budding feminist whose sisters worked inside and outside the home. She felt inferior to them, even though she had twice as many children to raise. Now she was rising up in perfect pace with the women's movement.

On the other hand, Dad was so sure his wife would love the opportunity to remodel the large, two-story house that he didn't think twice when he signed the papers and bought that dream house on Green Street. Think *Better Homes and Gardens.*

"You will love it, Afton! It's the perfect house," my father continued. "It's a white, two-story house with four bedrooms, a family room, and a large yard with a white, picket fence in the back. And...it's a block away from the gas station. It's such a good deal, we can afford to make it ours with a little remodeling!"

Mom, who was pregnant with her sixth child, didn't hold back. She lashed out at him.

"Jim, I'm sorry but I'm not happy about this at all!" she yelled.

"Why couldn't we have looked around together to find a house we both like? This is the second house you bought without any input from me. It doesn't work well if a couple can't discuss things and make decisions together when they're raising a family. The first time, I just went along with it. Not this time."

From that day on, my mother carried the pain of that move around with her like a constant companion. She left many of the moving boxes in the basement, unopened. Fifty years later, the boxes were still there, in that dark, damp, cellar—a reminder of how she had been evacuated from her "home sweet home." Although she had unconsciously buried her anger in that cold cellar, it was not so simple. Mom's anger resurfaced in other ways. One of her common complaints had to do with my brother's stamp collection.

"There was a rift between Anne and me because I know her boys stole stuff from our basement," she said to me one day. "They would come to my house and when they left, there would be stuff missing. They slowly stole Frank's valuable stamp collection. One day, the boys walked away laughing and I heard one of them say, 'See, I can just take anything. There is so much stuff down here you would never notice!'"

How did she know they actually stole the stamp collection? Did she go down into the cellar as soon as they left to search for evidence?

I wondered but I never asked. Always the peacemaker.

Whenever my father walked in the door after working long hours at the gas station, I was thrilled. My heart was full of joy. He gave each of us a big hug, always happy and smiling, even though I'm sure he was exhausted.

One day, Dad came home from work early. He was limping. There had been an accident at the gas station and his leg was red and swollen. He could barely walk. The rest of the family scrambled around the house, worried about him. After what seemed like a moment in time, an ambulance arrived. The paramedics put Dad on a stretcher and wheeled him out of the house. As the sirens screamed, I was speechless. I couldn't control my fear or my tears. Suddenly, my big, strong father was totally helpless. And so was I. I had no idea what had happened and I wasn't sure whether he would ever come home from the hospital. I ran upstairs into my blue bedroom, crying and praying.

"Please, God, save my father. Don't let him die."

The day the ambulance arrived at our house, my father was 45 years old. I was 16. His father, Grandpa K., died in the hospital after his appendix ruptured. He was just 56 years old. At that time, I was 8.

My father was diagnosed with Phlebitis. He had suffered a deep vein thrombosis (DVT) in his leg and (I believe) a Pulmonary Embolism from a blood clot had traveled to his lung. Luckily, he survived. When he came home from the hospital, we learned what had happened. He had been checking something under the hood of a car when suddenly, the car rolled toward him, pinning him against the wall. It turned out the car's emergency brake wasn't engaged. His employees immediately backed up the car and freed him. Then, they insisted he go home and rest.

That day is indelible in my memory. Although it wasn't the end of my father's life, it was the end of life as I knew it on 2498 Green Street. That day was the beginning of the end for my parents' marriage.

"You need to manage your employees from a desk," said the doctor. "Standing on cement floors is risky for you given your condition."

"I can't imagine sitting behind a desk," my father insisted, as he thought about his delicate situation. "I love the work—not the paperwork."

Eventually, he decided to lease his beloved Nibley Park Service Station to a family friend and look for another career. With a large family, he was open to any job he could find, even if it was temporary. The first opportunity he found was in maintenance at a manufacturing plant—a position my mother argued was beneath him.

"You have your own business and now you're mopping floors! Can't you find a better job than that?" Not only was my mother embarrassed for him, she was embarrassed for herself.

My father's decision to put family first stuck with me. When Bill, our first child, was a year old, Jim and I were both unemployed. It was the holiday season, so I found a part-time job at Auerbach's, my first employer. That year, I learned the fine art of gift wrapping, a skill I would never have learned with my English degree.

Dad's new job also meant he was home on weekends and he didn't have to work long hours, which added more stress to an already strained relationship between my parents. Eventually, Dad found a career opportunity. He took a job as a traveling salesman for a wholesale heating and air conditioning company. It was the perfect opportunity for him because he loved road trips and his work took him on paid personal road trips through the natural beauty of the four corners area—Utah, Arizona, Colorado, and New Mexico. It also offered him a break from Mom's anxiety when he was traveling.

The first time I saw "Death of a Salesman," I cried some giant tears. Watching Willy Lowman descend into a silent depression after losing his job was like watching my family on stage, but my mother was the one who became depressed after my father made the difficult decision to walk away from the business he loved for the sake of his own health.

I was a junior in high school when Mom had a fainting spell in the living room. Though this wasn't the first time it had happened, it was the first time I saw it happen. Dad took her to Holy Cross Hospital and, by the time they arrived, the doctors could find nothing physically wrong with her. However, as she was being evaluated, her primary doctor recommended a psychological assessment. The diagnosis: Depression.

That day was the beginning of a new reality for my mother—and for me. Most of the details have escaped my memory, but at that time in my life, as a high school student, I was called upon to care for my four sisters so I channeled the inner strength of my living grandmother, Grandma Kyriopoulos. Though the older girls were pretty independent, I was there if they needed anything and we all pitched in to take care of Jami, the youngest among us.

Mom resisted vehemently, begging her doctor to release her, but she was already in the hospital after having fainted in the living room. The doctor was concerned enough to transfer her to the psychiatric wing and the psychiatrist assigned to treat her recommended that she stay in the hospital for more intensive psychotherapy. Mental illness runs in my mother's family and with this news, Mom became even more angry.

Each day after school, I drove to the hospital to visit her. It was strange to see her so vulnerable. She had always been a strong woman, willing to stand up for what she believed was right. Sensing her reaction to the whole situation, I hid my mother's condition from my friends, who were worried about her.

"She's still at the hospital. They're doing a bunch of tests and trying to figure out why she keeps fainting," I said whenever someone asked how she was doing.

Mom insisted her psychiatrist was a cold, heartless man.

"He's rough with me. Just like your dad! He shakes me to wake me up if I happen to sleep through my scheduled appointment," she said. "I need to get out of here, Margie. He thinks I should get electroshock therapy! That is not going to happen!"

That therapy was a scary thought for me as well.

"I'm sorry to hear that, Mom," I said. Then, I changed the subject. "Let's go to the craft room and work on a boondoggle bracelet."

I was worried about her, but I didn't know what else to do or say. We walked down the hall and over to the craft room together, arm in arm, Mom in her hospital gown and me in my school clothes. I looked straight ahead and pretended not to hear the other patients moaning and groaning in their rooms. Even though it was a most uncomfortable place for a teenager to be, I needed to be there for my mother.

Once she was admitted to the psych ward, Mom was not allowed to release herself from the hospital. Three men had total control over her—her primary doctor, the psychiatrist, and my father. No wonder she was angry. Thanks to her strong will, she managed to avoid the electroshock therapy as a treatment for her clinical depression. She spent a few weeks in the hospital, lobbying to get out and growing increasingly angry with Dad for not signing the release form. Finally, my father signed the form and brought her home. Her primary doctor prescribed Phenobarbital. I'm not sure why, but it seemed to help with her anxiety.

After that trip to the hospital, if Mom ever fainted again, I'm sure she was not about to tell anyone. Did the memory of that trip to the hospital keep her from seeking medical help for the seizures she experienced later in her life? And, were her fainting spells actually seizures? Another family mystery.

After my mother's hospital stay, things between my parents got progressively worse. Whenever Dad was late coming home from work, tired and exhausted, Mom went out of her way to ignore him. As soon as she heard my father at the door, even if she had been enjoying the evening with us, she got busy cleaning or picking up around the house. Instead of greeting her husband with a loving hug, she pretended not to notice his arrival.

My parents separated for a few years and went to marriage counseling, but it didn't work for them. Dad moved in with our cousin who was divorced. A few months later, he was able to move back into our family's first home on 9th East after the tenants moved out. Meanwhile, my mother was determined to get her fair share.

"Your father wanted the divorce, so I finally found a lawyer," she said to me. She initiated the divorce and hired seven lawyers, one by one, until she found a lawyer who would fight for what she wanted—both family homes and the four-plex— a settlement for having been a wife and the mother of six children for 28 years.

Mom had become a stubborn, bitter woman who shared her anger with me every time we were together—before and after the divorce. I loved both of my parents, so it was difficult to listen to her anger toward my father.

Ultimately, she was awarded all of their joint property and Dad was able to keep his business property. It didn't make sense to me that he couldn't keep one of the family homes, but she was persistent. As I watched the long, painful process, I vowed never to follow in her footsteps.

My father, who was essentially evicted from our first family home, moved into an apartment nearby, relieved it was all over and pleased that he was able to keep the property he and his brother Ernie had inherited. He accepted his fate and started his life over again in his fifties. After all the turmoil, my father was ready for a new reality. He simply moved forward, eventually buying and selling a few properties, a mobile home, and a condo in Southern Utah. He also partnered with a couple of other men to invest in a 4-acre piece of land in Heber Valley. He called the property "Kyriopoulos Mountain."

Meanwhile, Mom became an instant landlord with a huge house, a rental home and a four-plex. It was a lot of work for a single woman and she did much of it herself. Although she became a realtor, managing all her own properties and spending time with her children and grandchildren kept her busy. Her family was always her highest priority.

"Work, work, work," as Uncle George had said.

For Christmas that year, I created two huge photo albums. Both were labeled, "Memories." I personalized each album (one for Mom and one for Dad) with photos and quotes. Each photo album was an individual Christmas gift for my divorced parents, a labor of love. I embellished the photo albums with quotes to highlight my own perceptions of their immigrant families and our family.

When Dad opened his photo album, he smiled and gave me a big hug, grateful for all the memories.

When Mom opened her scrapbook, she couldn't stop crying, so she closed the photo album and put it down. The past was just too much for her to re-live. I sat there, watching her sob, confused and hurt by her reaction. Over time, I forgave my mother, whose heart was heavy for a very long time.

As Mom grew older, she spent a lot of time in her bedroom. It had become her cocoon, her refuge. Recent photographs of her grandchildren were proudly displayed in every available space in her bedroom: on the walls, on top of the dresser and its matching vanity, and on top of the extra chest of drawers. Newspapers and books were stacked on the bed, on the floor, and in bookshelves. Her bedroom was a library full of memories.

The little two-drawer, cardboard nightstand next to her huge king-sized bed was draped with a white, crocheted doily (handmade by her mother). A glass of water, bottles of pills, a jar of Pond's face cream, and a tube of soft red lipstick were precariously balanced on that small nightstand. Both cardboard drawers were full of old photographs, cards, and letters from her children and grandchildren. From time to time, she opened up the top drawer and reread a few greeting cards. My father's black and white photographs were mostly stuffed into the bottom drawer, a visual archive of our life as a family.

MY FATHER'S PHOTOGRAPHS

I am fascinated
by his photographs,
stuffed away in dusty drawers,
waiting for me to pick them up,
one by one.

It's my father,
the photographer,
who draws me there,
as I slip into my parents' bedroom,
kneel down in prayer pose,
and open the bottom dresser drawer,
where I find myself,
cradled in my mother's arms.

She is smiling back at him
like she'll be there forever—
as though the photograph is enough
to keep them together.

CRAZY

~

JIM IS THE only adopted child in his family. He grew up with an older sister, a younger sister, and a little brother. Although his parents already had a child, they adopted him from the Children's Service Society in Salt Lake City.

"I think we should adopt a baby," he said to me one day.

"Really? We already have a happy, healthy, three-year old son. Why would we adopt a baby?"

Did he want to adopt a baby because he was adopted?

A few months later, I realized I was pregnant and the question didn't come up again. We were focused on the baby.

Jim's father, a professor of Economics at the University of Utah, was planning a sabbatical where he would be teaching at a US military base in Wiesbaden, Germany, and his parents had invited us to move into their house while they were living abroad.

"Being in a home instead of an apartment would be good for your family now that you are expecting another baby," Jim's mother said.

"Thank you so much," I said. Although I wanted a home of our own, we were struggling financially and I was planning to leave my teaching job for a couple of years to care for our new baby.

Once we settled in at his parents' home, a family came to look at the old blue sedan they had asked us to sell for them. It was the first Saturday of August 1975. Jim went out for a test drive with the couple who, for some reason, left their daughter behind. When I heard the chubby little 5-year old outside, sobbing, I realized she had climbed up into the flowering plumb tree.

"Help!" she cried. "I can't get down."

Oh my. I walked down the back stairs to help. She was stuck halfway up the tree, so I extended my right hand to lend a little support for her to jump down. Instead of taking my hand, she threw both her arms around my neck and jumped on top of me. Right on top of my baby.

Ouch!

Later that night, I felt a few contractions, so I called the emergency number for my doctor's office. The on-call doctor recommended bed rest.

"You need to rest now," he said. "Don't get up for anything. Just stay in bed and let your husband wait on you! Call the hospital if your contractions continue or get worse."

I was disappointed and worried, but hopeful that everything would be okay after a good, long rest. Luckily, it was a weekend. The next day was Sunday, August 3, 1975. My contractions were gone and I was relieved because we had been planning to go to the First Annual Arts Festival in Salt Lake City on the lawn of the State Capitol. We decided to go. It was a beautiful day to wander through the small event. There were colorful paintings, hand thrown pottery, photographs from all over the state, and handmade jewelry all on display under tents. Bill was enjoying the children's art projects—drawing, building blocks, and face painting while Jim and I strolled through the artists' displays and listened to live folk music. Suddenly, a rush of water poured down my legs.

"Jim, I am not sure what's happening, but I can't control it. I think my bladder is leaking."

"Oh no...You need to get back into bed. Let's go home and call the doctor."

The three of us headed back to our burgundy convertible, a hand-me-down from Jim's parents. I was wet and worried, but happy Bill had time to get his face painted like a tiger before we had to leave. He was having a good time at the Kid's tent.

As soon as we got back to Jim's parent's house, I called the emergency number again. This time, we were told to get to the hospital immediately. I realized this was serious and I was really scared. My baby wasn't due for another six weeks and my mother was vacationing in Greece with my three youngest sisters. They were visiting my brother and his family who were stationed in Crete with the Air Force. I called my sister Kathy.

"Kathy, I need to get to the hospital. I'm not sure what's happening. I'm leaking fluid and it's too early for me to be in labor."

"Oh no. I'm so sorry, Margie. I can help you. Can you bring Bill over here? Stephanie is asleep."

"Of course. Thank you so much."

We rushed Bill to Kathy's house and headed for the University of Utah Hospital. Neither of us had any idea what would happen next and I was still leaking what seemed like buckets of water. Once we got to the hospital, it all happened too fast. A doctor came in to examine me.

"Marjorie, your water has broken," he said. "There is a huge risk of infection now. It's a bigger risk to wait than it is to deliver your baby now."

Then, I got another big surprise.

"Dr. Warenski is out of town, so I will be delivering your baby. We will need to induce labor."

Now I was sobbing.

What about all those Lamaze classes and the natural birth I had been planning ever since I found out I was pregnant? This was the opposite of what I had imagined for the birth of my second child.

I was terrified and nervous, unable to breathe deeply. Instead, I hyperventilated. The nurse stayed by my side and tried to calm me.

"Try to relax," she said as she injected something into the IV.

"Hey, Dad," she said to Jim. "Go put on a gown and some gloves so you can be here for your baby's birth."

That was not what Jim had in mind. He was more nervous than I was. Back then, it was optional for fathers to be in the delivery room. He hadn't been there for Bill's birth and this little baby was coming way too soon. I was glad the nurse was able to convince him to be there for me and the baby.

Once the contractions started coming, I fought each one. I was totally out of synch with my body. I knew how to breathe, but I was doing it all wrong. To top it off, my baby wasn't ready to leave the warmth of my womb yet either. She was fighting against coming out into the world. What a scene it was! None of us were ready! It was a traumatic time for all of us!

"I think it's a little boy," said the nurse. "The baby's heartbeat is slow."

Before ultrasounds were routine, it was believed a heartbeat slower than 140 beats per minute was probably a male, while a faster heartbeat was probably a female.

After five or six hours of trying to breathe with the contractions instead of against them, the final push came and our tiny little 4-pound 6-ounce girl arrived, kicking and screaming to introduce herself to us!

I breathed a deep sigh of relief.

"It's a girl!" said the nurse, who was convinced I was delivering a baby boy.

She's alive, I thought. My baby girl was the same size as my first baby doll.

That day is a blur in my mind, although I remember being happy to have delivered a healthy baby girl and sad that she had to be rushed away immediately to an incubator.

In those days, women stayed in the hospital for a few days after delivering a baby and I was determined to extend my stay even longer.

Although I was able to nurse her when she was hungry, she had to stay in the incubator the rest of the time.

"I'm not ready to go home," I said to the nurse on my fourth day in the hospital. "I want to stay until I can take my baby home with me."

The next morning, the nurse came into my room and delivered the bad news. I had to leave the hospital even though my baby wasn't ready to go home.

"Your baby needs to stay here. Even though she is back to her birth weight, we need to continue monitoring her until she weighs at least 5 pounds."

"But...I want to stay here with my baby so I can breast feed her."

"I'm sorry, Marjorie," said the nurse. "We can't let you stay here. You can pump your breasts and bring the milk here so we can feed her your breast milk."

I was emotionally exhausted and sad. The nurse encouraged me to visit the hospital any time and as often as I wanted. Of course, timing wasn't always perfect—a big disappointment for me—but at least I was able to hold my tiny little girl dressed in the tiniest little onesie I had ever seen. Another strong little girl in the family!

I don't remember how I took care of Bill or how often Jim came to the hospital with me. Clearly, I was focused on bonding with my new baby.

I sent a telegram to my mother and sisters, who were still in Greece, accidentally transposing her birth weight as 6 pounds 4 ounces. That was a serendipitous blessing because my mother could enjoy her vacation in Greece with no worries about her premature granddaughter.

Finally, after a week, we were able to bring our 5-pound baby girl home. I was overwhelmed with joy, despite a lingering postpartum depression. Jim was working full time for Salt Lake County. He was also a full-time student, determined to graduate from the University of Utah ten years after he began. He took night classes at the University of Utah and studied at the library on weekends. He was rarely home.

Shadows of my mother's phone call lingered in my mind.

"Where is Jim? It's late! Is he having an affair?"

"No, Mom. He works on Tuesday evenings," I said, trying to ignore her trust issue.

I couldn't ignore my mother. Finally, one day I asked Jim whether he was having an affair with his married co-worker.

"You're crazy!" he said.

I wanted to believe it was all in my head. I wanted to believe he wasn't having an affair when he went off on his business trips or overnight fishing trips. Yet, somewhere deep inside me, I knew it was true. Eventually, his response was my inspiration for seeing a therapist. I remember that day, 45 years ago, like it was yesterday. It started out like any other day at that time of my life.

My breasts were full. I lifted my sweater, pulled down the flap of my nursing bra, and tried to breastfeed little Lizzie, but she was restless. She didn't want my milk. I carried her into the kitchen and prepared a bottle of Similac® with warm tap water. My doctor insisted there was no need to sterilize the water even though my mother believed it was necessary. I followed the doctor's advice.

Slowly, I walked back to my rocking chair and sat down, holding Lizzie in the crook of my left arm. I propped the bottle next to my breast and fed her as though I was nursing her. Finally, she was happy and relaxed. She drank the whole bottle and fell asleep in my arms. Before I got up, I glanced at my photo of the Golden Gate, remembering that San Francisco summer. Then, I checked the clock on the wall. I had an hour and a half to get ready for my therapy appointment.

I made a fresh pot of coffee in our Presto electric percolator and left the opened coffee can on the beige Formica countertop. As I waited for my coffee to finish brewing, I held Lizzie tightly against my chest, nervously patting her back and hoping there would be no colic. Once the coffee stopped percolating, I poured myself a cup and grabbed the cream out of the refrigerator. I poured cream into my coffee and some of the cream spilled on the counter.

Oh well. I'll clean that up later, I thought. Why don't I have the energy to finish the simplest tasks?

I had always been able to multi-task. I carried my coffee cup over to the kitchen table and sat down. A quiet house was a rare moment back then. I finished my coffee and walked down the hall to the nursery and gently placed Lizzie in her crib so I could get ready for my therapy appointment. Then, suddenly, the tears came on. I had no control over them. They just rolled down my face for no apparent reason.

It's not normal to be blue for this long, I thought.

I knew all about postpartum blues. I was blue for a day or two after Bill was born. This was different. It had been going on for months. But why? I had a good life—two beautiful children, a handsome husband, and a comfortable place to call home. I had everything to be happy about.

It was time to bathe my baby. I put the baby tub into the bathtub and ran the water, checking to make sure it wasn't too hot. Then, I picked Lizzie up and gently lowered her tiny pink body into her little bathtub. She smiled up at me, splashing around in the water. As I held onto her, I felt a flash of pure joy. In a world where everything else in my life seemed disconnected, my connection with our two beautiful children carried me through each day. I dressed her in a pink and white polka dot onesie, bundled her up in a blanket, and placed her carefully into her baby carrier on the floor.

I grabbed my Levi's and lay down on the bed, flat on my back, zipping my overgrown stomach into my jeans. Then, I went looking for a sweater to hide my "baby fat." Finally, I pulled my favorite ruby red sweater over my head and glanced at myself in the mirror. Success! My body was ready to go.

There was no time to think about my decision to see a therapist. No time to get anxious about what I would say. I had barely enough time to get to the clinic. On the way there, I drove to Mindy's house. She had offered to watch little Lizzie for me. Our kids were about the same age and we had been friends since before our children were born. By the time I arrived at my friend's house, Lizzie had fallen asleep. I carried her quietly up to the door and rang the bell.

"I'll be back in about an hour and a half," I whispered to Mindy, who waved me off.

I walked back to my car and drove to the clinic, which was located in a big, old house near 5th East and 27th South—not far from where I grew up. Slowly, I made my way up the stairs to the front porch and opened the front door. A young woman in a baby blue dress with flowing blonde hair, smiled at me. She looked a little like my Guardian Angel.

"Can I help you?"

"Yes," I said, softly. "I have an appointment with Kay."

"You must be Marjorie. Please make yourself comfortable. I'll let her know you're here. Would you like some coffee or tea?" she asked.

"No, thanks. I'm fine."

I settled into an overstuffed, olive sofa in what had once been a living room. Its huge arms and small wooden legs reminded me of my grandmother's sofa. I picked up a section of the Salt Lake Tribune from the coffee table in front of me. A story on the front page screamed out for my undivided attention.

Weirdo Invades Home — Dons Lingerie, Totes Gun

BURBANK, Calif. (AP) — A couple who took a skiing trip last weekend say they returned home to find a rifle-toting, lingerie-clad invader who had rearranged furniture, emptied perfume bottles, and scribbled notes about the president and Sally Field.

Jeffrey Hill overpowered the intruder and locked him in the trunk of the family car until police arrived Sunday night, but memories of the man's bizarre behavior in their home may make the house unliveable for her family, Olivia Hill said Wednesday.

The man, who identified himself to police as Richard Roe, 45, of Arizona, was booked for investigation of attempted murder, burglary and possession of a deadly weapon.

Roe pleaded innocent to all three counts during arraignment Thursday in Municipal Court. His preliminary hearing was set for Feb. 27.

The Hills left Jan. 16 for a four-day trip to Big Bear Lake to celebrate Mrs. Hill's 30th birthday.

When they returned Sunday night, "We walked into the kitchen dumbfounded. We knew something very strange was going on," said Hill, 38.

Notes were taped to the kitchen cabinets, including some that said: "My name is Sally Field," "Ronald Reagan is the head of state," and "All ye who enters these doors shall sink into the bowels of the earth." A red candle was burning in the living room.

Police Detective Craig Ratliff said he was in touch with the FBI "because of the note the guy wrote about Reagan."

"Olivia, my wife, immediately ran with our 2-year-old son, Hunter, down to a neighbor's house to call 911," said Hill. "I continued moving through the house alone."

He confronted the intruder in a darkened doorway. "I shouted, 'Who are you and what . . . are you doing in my house?'"

"He just brought the rifle up with his left hand and pointed it at me. . .

"I lunged forward, grabbed the barrel of the gun, and we both fell to the floor," said Hill, who stands 6-foot-1 and weighs 225 pounds. He said he pounded the man in the face. "And then he finally said, 'OK, OK.'"

Hill described the man as a "Charles Manson-type of guy with long, filthy, wild-looking hair." Hill marched the man out to the family car and locked him in the trunk.

"I can't touch anything in this house because this man violated us," Mrs. Hill said. "I don't know if I can stay here again."

While there, the man "changed into my underwear, police think, at least a dozen times a day," she said.

"He loved my clothes, and he loved order," she added.

"For example, he threw out all odd pieces of silverware and crystal. He threw out every bottle of liqueur but put every bottle of hard liquor into the refrigerator. He threw out the frozen steaks and the frozen shrimp, but he put all the rest of the frozen food into a bathroom medicine chest," she said.

"He tried making waffles from Rice Chex. He threw out all my junk jewelry, but wrapped my expensive jewelry in his clothes. And then he emptied out every bottle of my perfume onto his clothes, and then neatly stored them in a bundle under a living room window seat."

Now that's crazy!

Before I could finish reading the story, Kay was standing in front of me.

"Good Afternoon, Margie," she said softly. "It's good to see you. My office is just down the hall."

"Uh...Thanks. It's good to see you, too." Only my mother and close friends call me Margie.

I followed Kay through the living room and down the hall, past the former family's bedrooms to another former bedroom at the end of the hall. She closed the door behind me and motioned for me to sit in the black leather love seat facing her desk.

"How are you doing today, Margie?" she asked.

"Okay. I mean, I don't know... I'm confused. And I cry all the time."

"I see... Well, why don't you tell me a little about what's happening for you right now."

I began by talking about Jim, trying to avoid talking about myself.

"Well, my husband is working full-time and taking a full load of classes at the University. He is never home."

Kay interrupted me gently.

"How about you? What do you like to do for fun?"

"Me? Well, I like to take photos. And, I used to write poetry. But I don't have any energy these days."

I felt the familiar tears coming on and tried to hold them back. Kay handed me a whole box of Kleenex. I pulled out a tissue and wiped my eyes.

I'd love to read your poetry sometime," Kay said.

"You would?"

"Yes. I would. Now, tell me more about what's happening for you."

I grabbed another Kleenex, embarrassed by my uncontrollable sobbing as I looked out the window — away from Kay's face.

"It's alright to cry in here. I have plenty of Kleenex."

I shifted my body around and crossed my legs trying to find a comfortable position. More tears. More Kleenex. The hour passed before I knew it and I cried the whole time as I described what led me there. Through my tears, I talked mostly about the shock of a labor-induced delivery and the time my husband had said I was crazy when I asked him whether he was having an affair.

Kay glanced at the small clock on her desk and said, "I'm so sorry, Margie. I have another appointment, but I'd like for us to meet again. How does next week sound?"

"Okay," I said, as I looked down at the ancient Persian rug on the floor and studied the design.

"Is this a good time for you?" She asked.

"I think so. I need to check with my friend who's helping me out today."

"Okay. Just let me know if you need to change or cancel. Otherwise, I'll see you in a week," she said. "Oh, yes. Before you leave, would you please complete one more form for me? It's confidential, but we need it for our records."

I completed the form quickly and handed it back to her.

Kay glanced at the form and said, "I notice you left the space next to 'Occupation' blank."

"Should I have written housewife?" I asked sarcastically.

"How about writer? Or photographer?" She said in an inquiring tone.

Kay handed the form back to me and I decided to add "Writer" as my occupation. Before leaving her office, I pulled a few more tissues out of the box and put them in my coat pocket.

"Thank you," I said, embarrassed to be in this situation but grateful for the opportunity to talk with someone.

"You're welcome. Have a good weekend."

I walked toward the front door, looking straight ahead to avoid eye contact with the people in the waiting room.

In the privacy of my car, more tears flowed and I wiped them away with Kay's Kleenex. Snowflakes were falling softly. As I drove, I felt like I was inside my favorite snow globe—the one with a tiny snowman wearing black top hat and holding a bright red balloon. Over the years, I've probably spent hours watching the snow fly around inside that little glass globe, amazed at how real it looks.

I drove to Mindy's house to pick up little Lizzie. She greeted me at the front door.

"Hi, Margie. Isn't the snow beautiful? Can you stay and join me for a cup of coffee?"

"I'd love to, Mindy, but I need to pick up Bill from preschool."

"Okay. Maybe next time."

"Sounds good. In fact, do you think you could watch Elizabeth again next week?"

"Of course. She is such a sweet little baby. I can't wait until the summer when our kids will be playing outside together!"

"Yes. That will be great!" I said as I reached down to pick up little Lizzie in her carrier.

"Thanks again. I really appreciate your help."

"No problem at all. I hope to see you at the Mommy and Me class on Friday. It sounds like a good program."

"Yes. It does. See you then," I said, as I walked out the door.

I drove to Bill's preschool to pick him up and we headed for home. Everything seemed so normal. When we got home, Jim was watching the news on TV.

"How was your day?" he asked, eyes staring at the screen in front of him.

"Okay. I went to see Kay."

"Oh, yeah. I forgot about that. How'd it go?"

"She wants to see me again next week."

"Hi there, buddy," he said to Bill. "Come sit with Dad and tell me all about your day."

I carried Lizzie to the bedroom and changed her diaper, trying not to notice the boxes and wrapping paper still stacked in the corner of the room since the belated baby shower two weeks earlier. Then, I carried her back into the living room and sat in my father-in-law's big brown recliner, both children in my lap.

Bill, Elizabeth and Me, 1975

"Did you hear the news?" Jim asked. "Senator Ted Kennedy is coming to town and I have tickets to the fundraiser!"

"Oh...no...I must have missed it."

Jim often avoided any deep conversation with me by talking about the news.

That night, I dreamt I was wandering through the house when I noticed this large, tomb-like structure in the middle of the kitchen. There was a woman standing inside a structure in the middle of the kitchen. She was beautiful. She was perfect. She looked like a goddess. The woman stepped down and began slowly walking around the house. I looked back into the kitchen and suddenly, another woman appeared. This woman seemed more human. Her hair was flowing freely as she wandered around the house. The second woman seemed more alive than the first woman and she seemed happier. For some reason, I was afraid of her. She seemed so...real.

A week flew by quickly, and soon, it was time for my next appointment with Kay. I thought about canceling, but I resisted the urge and once I was in Kay's office, I shared my dream with her.

"Though I'm just speculating, I wonder whether both of these women are you," she said.

I felt the familiar tears starting to fall.

'Me? I'm afraid of myself?' I thought.

"Where did your tears come from?" asked Kay, matter-of-factly.

"I don't know. Maybe I'm afraid of needing you. Afraid of needing Jim. Afraid of needing anyone!" was my reaction.

"It's okay to need me right now, Margie. You won't need me forever. And it's okay to need Jim. He needs you, too. We all need each other."

"Well, he doesn't act like he needs me! When we got married, I thought we would share everything with each other. He treats me the same way he treats a stranger on the street. I have no idea how he feels about me. I feel like I'm just another random person in his political life," I said.

Then she asked me a personal question..."How is your sex life with Jim?"

"Our sex life?" I asked, surprised.

"Yes. Often, when a couple is having problems, their sex life reflects those problems."

"Oh, that's not true for us. We've never had problems with sex."

Well, sometimes I wish it was better.

I told Kay about my summer in San Francisco and the decision I made to marry Jim, concluding that, in the end, I did the sensible thing.

"The sensible thing?" she asked.

"Yes. Donald was sensitive, but Jim was so sensible."

"So, you thought you had to choose between sensitive and sensible?" she asked.

"Yeah...I guess so."

Kay glanced at the small clock on her desk. "I'm sorry we have to stop here, Margie. I have another appointment. I hope you have a good weekend. Do you have any plans?"

"Plans? No plans."

"Well, I hope you have a good weekend anyway. See you next week."

"Yeah, thanks." I said.

As I drove away, I thought about how Jim and I never seemed to have any plans for the weekend.

As I drove to Mindy's house, I wondered whether it was time to tell her where I was going every week. Once I was inside, I started with small talk, as usual.

"Was everything okay?" I asked her.

"Of course! Lizzie is a wonderful baby. She's never a problem. She's taking a nap right now. How about a cup of coffee?"

"Sure. That sounds nice," I said. "Thanks so much."

I followed Mindy into the kitchen and sat down at the table, watching her measure the coffee and turn on her Mr. Coffee machine.

"There's something I need to tell you," I said, softly. "I've been seeing Kay, the therapist you invited to our Mommy and Me class. That's where I go every Friday."

"Good for you! She has helped me a lot. In fact, I still see her once in a while. I call it my reality therapy."

Mindy poured the coffee and carried the two mugs to the table.

"Believe me, you're not alone. I'm just glad you were able to share that with me," said Mindy. "If you ever need to talk, I'm here."

"Thanks so much, Mindy. I really appreciate your help. I don't know what I'd do without you."

"No problem at all. Hey, we're going skiing tomorrow. Would you and Jim like to join us?" she asked.

"Uh, thanks. But I think Jim has to study tomorrow."

Soon, I was meeting with Kay on a weekly basis. At some point, I brought a couple of poems with me. I told Kay how I usually wrote my best poems when I was sad.

"Thank you so much," she said. "I'm looking forward to reading this and I hope someday, when you are no longer sad, you'll still be able to write poetry. Before we get started, I need to tell you something. Based upon our work together so far, I have diagnosed you as clinically depressed. I'm happy to work with a medical doctor to prescribe some medication for you if you'd like. Also, I think we should meet twice a week."

Hmmm...How can she tell I'm clinically depressed? I wondered.

"I don't really want to take any drugs," I said. "My mother used to take Phenobarbital for her anxiety and she would give me a pill sometimes. It just made me more anxious. And, I'm not sure I can afford to come twice a week."

"There is no need to take any medication. That is up to you. And, about adding more appointments, though it won't be forever, it will help with the healing process. I believe you qualify for financial assistance, so I'll give you some more paperwork for that before you leave."

'So...Jim was right. **I am crazy**,' I thought.

"Were you able to do anything fun last week?" Kay asked.

"Not really. We went to a party hosted by some of Jim's colleagues and I wanted to go home early, so Jim brought me home and he went back to the party without me. I couldn't believe it! My sister was babysitting for us and he didn't even drive her home. He just dropped me off and left. I decided to call my mom and ask her to take all of us, including the kids, to her house. When Jim got home, no one was there to greet him."

I can't believe I told Kay that story.

"Sounds like a little drama," she said.

"Yes. It was dramatic."

I didn't tell her about how he came to my mom's house to get us and how I slammed the car door so hard that glass shattered into the back seat where the children were sitting.

"Do you want to work on filing for a divorce?" Kay asked.

"No," I insisted. "I'm here to save my marriage!"

Although I was determined that my marriage wouldn't end in divorce like my parents' marriage, I didn't realize how I had followed my mother's footsteps blindly during much of my own failed marriage. Years later, I remembered how, like my mother, I rarely greeted my husband when he walked in the door, pretending to be busy. And, if he hadn't called to say he was going to be late, I punished him by either yelling at him or by ignoring him. No wonder he didn't call to tell me he was going to be late!

A few years later, after we were settled in to our new home, I learned the truth. I learned the truth on the night of the famous, annual spring Martini Bash, an event we attended every year along with hundreds of Salt Lake City's beautiful people. It was a huge social event held at a downtown hotel and sponsored by a wealthy young couple in the community. Martinis and fancy canapés flowed freely throughout the hotel. The whole place was reserved for this invitation-only event. The event is now, thankfully, a fundraiser.

While we were at the event, I was chatting with one of Jim's colleagues when, suddenly, he stopped talking and looked into my eyes.

"I can't help myself. I'm sorry, Margie. I need to tell you something. You are a sweet person who doesn't deserve to be treated like this. Do you know Jim is seeing another woman?"

"What?"

"I'm so sorry, Margie," he said again before he walked over to another group of people to socialize.

I felt like a fool as I sat there by myself surrounded by all those beautiful people. I tried to stay calm for the rest of the evening, but that was impossible. I just kept drinking cheap martinis and didn't eat enough canapés. I wasn't alone in drinking too much. I was alone in my own little world, singing along with Patsy Cline, "Crazy...crazy for feeling so blue...and I'm crazy for loving you."

Then I saw Jim across the room. He was motioning to me that it was time to go. I staggered toward him and we started walking through the hallway, side-by-side, to the hotel lobby. Suddenly, I stopped walking. Jim turned around to look at me.

"You liar!" I yelled.

Then, I surprised myself and lifted my shiny, red high-heeled foot and kicked him in the crotch. As he doubled over, I felt the stares, but at that moment, I didn't care about anyone else.

My husband had been having an affair and I felt like a fool.

I knew it was happening all along. I knew it from the day she smiled as she gave me that lovely handmade crib quilt. I knew it by the way she watched me from across the room. I knew it the day he denied the affair and told me I was crazy. I knew the day I slammed the car door so hard the window shattered into a million pieces. I knew it the day I plastered the bathroom mirror with images of Playmates clipped out of his Playboy magazines. I knew it the day I put my fist through the storm door and watched the glass fall down the front steps. That was the day I finally asked him to leave.

My pain poured out into a poem that flowed freely from my pen. I still wonder where it came from.

THE HUNTER

The hunter in him
wants me…
I am his prey,
his territorial claim,
his proof of power and wit.

He wants to own me for himself
to have and not hold,
a trophy in his glass house,
a monument added to his collection
of dead dreams.

"The Hunter" was not only published in *Network Magazine*, a local Feminist monthly publication, it was used jokingly at a Roast in honor of my ex-husband.

I now realize how my mother's anger at my father played out in my own marriage. I had made an unconscious pact with her. Despite my best intentions, I had followed her lead, carrying the trauma of the Deer Hunting Mishap in my own reactions when I felt most vulnerable. The trauma had passed on to my generation.

"It wasn't an accident."

"He had another wife."

"Where have you been?"

"Are you having an affair?"

I'm not sure which came first—the chicken or the egg—my depression or the affair. But the truth, eventually, came tumbling out. In the end, although I wasn't able to save our marriage, I was able to save myself.

After a year as a single parent, I traveled to Japan for a work project. It was a memorable trip, professionally and spiritually. I was there for seven weeks. Bill and Liz stayed with Jim and I called them every week at the same time to keep in touch. On weekends, I went shopping or visited temples and shrines with my colleagues (or alone).

One of our weekend sightseeing adventures was a trip to the Hase Kannon Temple in Kamakura. As we walked toward rows and rows of tiny shrines, I was overwhelmed with sadness. Slowly, I moved closer to the sea of baby statues, all dressed up in warm woolen capes. Visitors lay memorial gifts at the feet of these little shrines, called "Jizōs"—miniature teddy bears, flower arrangements, and pinwheels. Many of the Jizōs wore red, a protective color in East Asia. In fact, in Japan, the color red symbolizes healing, fertility, gestation, childbirth, infant death, children's limbo, and the unconnected dead.

Jizō Statues at the Hase Kannon Temple, Kamakura Japan, March 25, 1984

The story of the Jizō originates from the 14th-century tale of the Sai no Kawara ("riverbed of the netherworld"), a place much like the River Styx in Greek mythology or Purgatory in Christian tradition. According to legend, children who are miscarried, stillborn, or die before their parents enter into a limbo, or kind of hell, at the banks of a rocky river. There they are forced to build towers from stones to atone for the sin of causing such grief, and to help add to their parents' merit in the afterlife.

—FROM "JAPAN'S COLORFUL GRAVESTONE DECORATIONS PROTECT THE SOULS OF LOST CHILDREN" BY WILL KUAN, WWW.ATLASOBSCURA.COM, APRIL 6, 2017

In my unconscious memory, these little shrines are a memorial to all the babies and children in our family who were unborn, still born, or died before their parents.

HASE KANNON

Kamakura, Japan, March 1984

I am in a holy place,
A shrine,
A monument
To all who have known
The warmth of the womb.

The sea of baby faces
has one expression
and all I can hear is
the sound of
a million plastic pinwheels
whirling in the wind,
breathing life
into this kaleidoscopic mausoleum
where memories are wrapped
in carefully crocheted caps

and warm woolen sweaters—
bright red, pale pink, baby blue,
and lemon chiffon—
protecting each small child
from a chill in the air.

My life didn't get any better after our divorce. It was just different. I even considered the possibility of getting back together with Jim after my relationship with my second husband-to-be ended abruptly. That is another very long story.

One day, I called Jim and invited him to join me for a walk in the neighborhood. He accepted. We walked together past the homes of neighbors who often greeted us before we were divorced. At the time, I was oblivious to the fact that they might have been watching us as we strolled together past their houses.

"I've been thinking," I said. "Maybe we could try again."

He stopped walking and looked at me. He didn't say a word, but I could see it in his face. It was too late. He had moved on. And my intuition told me it was time for me to move on as well. We continued our walk across the street and down into the wooded "gully" where we used to go for walks with our children. He calmly listened to my story as we walked.

A week later, I went back to see Kay, afraid of descending into the depths of another depression. She gently reminded me that depression is different from sadness. I was very sad. But I was not going back into that inferno called depression.

PILGRIM

~

IN THE FALL of 1989, Unisys offered me a promotion, along with a relocation to Minnesota as manager of our group of technical writers based in Salt Lake City, Utah and Roseville, Minnesota. Liz was in 9th grade, beginning her first year of high school. Bill had just graduated from East High School and he was on his way to Montana State University in Bozeman.

Somehow, during a quiet conversation at Ruth's Diner, I convinced Liz to move with me instead of staying in Utah with her father.

"Liz, I would love it if you came with me to Minnesota. It would give us a chance to have time together one-on-one, which we have never had since the day you were born. It's your choice, but I believe it would be a good move for both of us. If it doesn't work out, you can always come back to Utah."

"Okay, Mom," she said.

From my perspective, she had agreed with me. Later I learned she felt like she didn't really have a choice. As parents, we have a huge influence on our children—more so than we realize.

It was a big move, but I was ready for a new adventure and looking forward to finally spending some quality time with my fourteen-year-old daughter. She blossomed in her new environment as a strong competitor in cross-country skiing and cross-country running! We spent most weekends together exploring the Twin Cities and she spent summers with her dad in Salt Lake City.

Three years after our move to Shoreview, Minnesota, I met the writer who became my second husband. I was no longer a rebellious young woman looking for a knight in shining armor to rescue me from my family. Instead, I became the rescuer. We met at a writing group where he was the group leader. My dad wanted to meet him.

"What do you have to offer my daughter?" My father asked.

"Nothing..." he responded.

Silence.

"My love," my fiancé finally responded.

That did not go over well with Dad, a practical man who was still paying alimony and had paid child support until all of his children were adults.

"Is that all you have to offer?" asked Dad.

This time he had no response.

Dad was not impressed. Although he did not approve of the marriage, he always accepted me —unconditionally.

Like two fools, despite my father's disapproval, we were married in 1993 in St. Paul, Minnesota. This time, I was sure I had found someone who would love me forever, someone who would go beyond his own pain to share a rich relationship with me.

Instead, three years later, I awoke from a dream in which I had just asked my second husband to leave.

"I can no longer live with the alcohol," my dreaming self said.

Drinking controlled his life and it interfered with ours. I was afraid to admit I had failed, once again, to make my marriage work.

The words of my friend Roger haunted me. "Margie, you could love anyone."

And my favorite Sherwood Anderson quote jumped out at me.

"I am a lover who has not found my thing to love."

I looked up at my guardian angel hanging on the wall. A gift from my mother. My guardian angel had seen it all happen. She saw us as we tried to cross that bridge of pain together and emerge as two whole people. She saw us fall into the river and struggle to survive, trusting me to let go of him and follow my own path. She helped me pull myself away from the current that had been dragging me downstream. My guardian angel knew I could no longer try to save this man from himself.

It was Sunday morning. The morning after another difficult day. The morning after we'd had another emotional blowout. I was in a panic. I had left my car overnight in a marginal neighborhood. He had been up all night, writing. I had to interrupt him and ask him to drive me to work. I thought about taking a taxi. Then I thought again. A taxi was too expensive. So, I decided to interrupt him. When I opened the door, the smell of beer hit me hard.

"I'm worried about my car," I said. Would you give me a ride to work?"

I had interrupted him once again, something he hated.

"Why are you so anxious?"

"I don't know. I just am."

I kept pushing him to hurry. Finally, I got into the driver's seat and waited for him. He came out to the garage and motioned for to me to move into the passenger seat. Nope. I was stubborn. He had been drinking all night and I was going to drive.

"You're so weird," he said.

"Really? You're the weird one!"

I blew up at him and the fight between us had climaxed by the time we got to my office, where I was relieved to find my car still in the parking ramp. Once I was calm, I wanted to calm the relationship but he was still angry.

For what? I wondered. For controlling his Saturday?

It's true. I had taken control again. Would I ever learn to let go? I even wanted to control which car he should drive home because I was afraid he wouldn't have enough gas money.

I worked at the office until 5:30 that night. Then, I drove home to get ready for Amy's party. When I got home, he was in his room, writing.

"Are you planning to go to the party with me?" I asked.

He got up, behaving like a two-year old, pouting as he got dressed. He seemed spaced out. I wasn't sure whether he was drunk or whether he was still in his writing mind. I now know the two went together. He started in on me, complaining about our relationship.

"Do you want to go to the party or not?" I asked calmly.

"Will you drive?" he asked.

"Sure."

"Well, I'm feeling pretty belligerent," he said.

"Well, I don't want to drive all the way to Northfield with a belligerent man. I'm not into that now. And I never will be," I said.

"I really don't want to go," he said.

"Fine. I'll go alone," I responded.

I drove around the block and came back, just in case he had changed his mind. When I got home, I went upstairs into his office.

"Are you sure you don't want to go?"

"I'm still upset about what had happened this morning. And, when I said I was feeling belligerent, I was talking about being belligerent at the party, not during the drive. It's still too long a drive to take with you."

"Fine. It's up to you. I want you to join me, but not if it means a fight all the way there and back."

I was looking forward to an enjoyable evening with friends.

"Okay. I'd rather stay home," he said.

"Thanks for being honest." I turned around, went downstairs and out to the car. Alone in the car on my way out of town, I turned up the music and drove in peace to Byerly's where I picked up some fresh daisies for Amy. It was her birthday and I wanted to give her the flower I most love to receive.

I took the scenic route, driving through the countryside to

Northfield, Minnesota, a place where I knew I would be comfortable. More comfortable than I was in my own home, which was no longer the refuge it used to be. "Home Sweet Home" was no longer sweet. I had lost my respect for the person I vowed I would love forever just a few years earlier. There were warning signs, but I had been in denial.

At the party, I was at home with friends and strangers, all of whom welcomed me with open arms. I simply told everyone that my husband had been up writing all night and he was already asleep for the night. It was a logical excuse.

I stayed for a couple of hours, socializing with Amy, her family, and her friends. It was relaxing and enjoyable. Thoughts about my marriage swirled around in my head during my solo drive home.

It's over, I thought.

For me, sadly, this is when I withdraw completely. I can only take so much. Then I curl up in a little ball and cry myself to sleep, hoping it will all be over in the morning.

When I got home, I went upstairs. He was still sitting at the computer. I ignored him, went into the bedroom, and closed the door. I needed a sweet retreat and I didn't want to ruin the evening.

A few days later, I asked him to find another place to live and work so I could get on with my own life's work. What did he do? He complained that I was taking away my own car. Yes, I was. I was taking back everything that was mine. My car, my heart, my soul, myself.

I began to examine the roots of my life's journey. In a few days, I would be driving my Toyota Camry to Salt Lake City to give it to Liz, who is grateful for every little thing I do. I was looking forward to spending time with her, my mom, and my sisters over Memorial Day weekend. I was also looking forward to interviewing my aunts and uncles about their lives growing up in Utah.

The long drive was a perfect way to spend some time thinking about my life and the direction I was taking. I had been thrown a curve ball and I didn't know whether to run for it or let it pass me by.

Driving through Iowa, millions of Monarch butterflies greeted me as they migrated north from Mexico. I was sure it was a sign of the changes I was making on my own journey. I took the first exit and stopped at a small town to watch the show, in awe of nature's beauty.

"Let it be...Let it be... Let it be..."

Suddenly, that song had even more meaning for me. I was desperate to find a place within myself where peace lives. I wanted to inhale and exhale that peace every moment for the rest of my life. I longed to get back to the love within me. A life where there is love around me and inside me. I was hungry for the love I see each time I look into Liz's face when she's teaching a yoga class, every time I watch Bill in action working on a project, and whenever my grandchildren smile back at me with their big brown eyes. My children and grandchildren are blessed with beautiful souls.

Love is strange. It takes you by surprise most of the time and then holds on to your heart. Sometimes it won't let go of you until it has destroyed you. I loved that man but my love for him was killing me. I had resisted giving myself what I had so freely given to him, whether he wanted it or not. I needed to let go of him and learn to love myself. Once again, the words flowed freely from my own pen.

THE LEECH

Like a leech, he attached himself to me
and I watched it all happen, slowly.
I was an observer, a photographer,
a distant participant
watching my heart's blood
pour into his work,
his dreams,
his desires.
I watched as he took it all—

my heart,

my soul,

my underwear.

He wanted to be like me,

said it was the highest form of love

but all I could see,

as I pulled away,

was the blood dripping off my body,

and all I could hear

was the sucking sound

of a leech in the north woods.

Once we separated, I realized he had been sleeping with another woman. He knew well how to break my monogamous heart. Although we had been together for five years, each of us had been traveling a separate, rocky road and it was time to end our feeble attempt to make it work. By the spring of 1998, we were divorced and I couldn't wait to ask the priest for an ecclesiastical divorce. In fact, I would have preferred an annulment, even though up to three ecclesiastical divorces are allowed in the Orthodox Church.

When I received my first ecclesiastical divorce, the priest had asked me about forgiveness and I thought about the day I selected the angel card, "Forgiveness," just before my move from Utah to Minnesota, knowing I needed to forgive Jim.

This time, I came prepared to meet the tribunal of priests. I told my story and all three priests looked at me, smiling in unison as the priest from Wisconsin gently recommended that, based on my history, I should probably listen carefully to my friends and family should I ever decide to marry again. As I left the church, I said a little prayer of forgiveness for myself and my ex-husband.

MOVING OUT

"Jesus, could the irony be that suffering forms a stronger
bond than love?"

—DAVID BOTTOMS

Is that why I find it so difficult to leave this place?
Is it because I made my own bed
and I must lie in it forever,
despite the fact that both of us sleep
in our own beds, alone,
coming together only when our loneliness is greater
than our fear of rejection?

I look around me and imagine the things I will take with me
when I leave this place:

The oak dresser I refinished by hand,
slowly transforming it from black to tan,
an antique that has moved with me
from Salt Lake City to Shoreview to Minneapolis,
and will join me in my new apartment in St. Louis Park
where I begin again, alone.

My Guardian Angel,
the one who watched over me when I was a child
with her flowing, blue gown and her huge, white wings
guarding a young girl and boy at night
as they walk across a raging river on a broken bridge.
My mother gave me that Guardian Angel three times.
The first time, she hung it on the pale blue walls of my bedroom;
the second time, she gave it to me for my 32nd birthday, just before my

first divorce;
and again, twenty years later, she sent me a pocket-sized mirror
with the same Guardian Angel printed on the back—
just in time for this move.

My photographs, pictures that document my life,
memory by memory,
since I bought my first 35mm camera at twenty-one.
I take my photographs with me wherever I go.
They remind me of my full life—52 years of love and suffering,
The photographs don't lie. They simply record events—
weddings, birthdays, graduations, trips to Japan, Paris, London,
Mexico, Greece—
reflecting, for better or worse, in sickness and in health,
the days of my life.

Framed pictures and prints that hang on every wall in this place,
more reminders of people and places I've known—
Charlie Chaplin, the "Writer and the West," the New Orleans Jazz
Festival,
the Full Moon shining down on twelve Native American women in
red,

a deep purple street in Zihuatanejo,
Eugene Smith's Studebaker on Dream Street.
I carry them with me as reminders that there's a time for every
season—
birth and death, tears and laughter,
mourning and dancing, love and hate,
war and peace.

Why am I unable to begin packing up my life again?
Why the inertia? When I think about being alone in my new place,
I smile inside. Still, I long for the kind of love
that keeps my soul whole and offers me peace.
This is what my history tells me—that I want to be in a place
where love outweighs the suffering.

Jesus, help me make this move smoothly.
Help me pack up my life's moments and leave this place
with love in my heart and a pocketful of Guardian Angels
to protect me whenever I walk through a storm at night
on another broken bridge.

There is a Buddhist principle called "from today onward" which affirms that, while we can't escape our past, we can be transformed by it in a way that strengthens the good in us. Now that I see everything through a new lens, I am able to allow a brighter, stronger version of myself to emerge—a woman who is compassionate toward herself and others in her life. A woman who builds lasting relationships with friends. A woman who leaves behind the depression, despair, and disappointment of past generations to lift her children and grandchildren up to the sun's warmth and light.

SUICIDE IS PAINLESS

~

MY MOTHER GATHERED our family's history together in the form of photographs and yellowed newspaper clippings tucked away in boxes. They were everywhere. When she died, my sisters sent them to me, at my request. At that time, I was living in Fairfax, Virginia.

A year later, I finally opened up one of the boxes. Like an archeologist, I sifted through the photos and papers, uncovering the artifacts. For the first time in my life, I saw photos of Aunt Wanda and her husband Bill on their wedding day, photos of my mother and her sisters, photos of my mother's family on the farm. She had preserved these artifacts by storing them in candy boxes, cookie tins, and even a faded, Auerbach's gift box.

As I picked up each of Wanda's wedding photos, I was getting to know the aunt I never knew, a young woman full of joy and happiness on her wedding day in 1947, the same year I was born. I found a professional, oval shaped photo of her wearing a white chiffon dress with a corsage made of three, large, white gardenias placed over her heart. Was it an engagement photo? A wedding photo? I picked it up and held it gently in my hand. Wanda **was** a beautiful woman.

Bill and Wanda, November 7, 1947

Portrait of Wanda

That portrait of Wanda took me back to a Memorial Day trip to the cemetery when I was a teen. As I held the photograph in my hand, I remembered that day. It was the day we realized the porcelain photo on Wanda's tombstone had been vandalized.

"It wasn't an accident," my mother had whispered, sobbing.

I still remember the image on Wanda's tombstone before that day. It was the same one I was holding in my hand.

I also uncovered some yellowed, roughly clipped newspaper stories in the same box. One of the clippings was Wanda's obituary. Another was a news story about the Deer Hunting Mishap. Both clippings were from the Salt Lake Tribune, October 17, 1948. Wanda is smiling in the obituary photo. She's wearing a large corsage with three gardenias on her chest—just like the one in the portrait. There was also a clipped newsprint photo of a somber Wanda wearing a stylish black dress.

Young S. L. Matron, 23, Killed in Rifle Mishap

A young Salt Lake woman, Mrs. Wanda Chause Clements, 23, 823 S. Main, was accidentally shot and killed Saturday while hunting in Diamond Fork canyon near Spanish Fork.

The bullet was fired accidentally from a gun held by her husband, William P. Clements, 24, who was just a few feet away.

Investigating officers said Mrs. Clements, her husband, and a friend Wesley Hughes, 21, also of Salt Lake City, had come through some brush onto the road when a deer was sighted to the east.

Mr. Clements began throwing a shell into the breech of his rifle preparatory to taking aim at the deer, when his wife reportedly spoke to him.

According to officers, he half turned to answer her and the gun fired. The bullet hit Mrs. Clements just below the heart. She died instantly.

Other hunters, including Lt. Charley Allred, Provo, Utah state highway patrol, were summoned immediately. Lt. Allred sent for Sheriff Theron S. Hall, County Atty. Arnold C. Roylance, both of Springville, and Deputy Sheriff Ruben Christiansen, Spanish Fork, who made the investigation.

Billie mountain is located in Diamond Fork canyon a branch of Spanish Fork canyon.

The couple, who had been married about a year, have no children. Mrs. Clements was born in Salt Lake City, Dec. 8, 1926, a daughter of Mr. and Mrs. William Chause. She was graduated from Granite high school in 1942.

She is survived by her parents, her husband, three sisters and two brothers, Mrs. Ann Lendaris, Mrs. Alice Hale, Mrs. Afton Kyripoulos, James, and George Chause, all of Salt Lake City.

She was married to Mr. Clements March 7, 1947, in Salt Lake City.

Mrs. Clements was a member of Greek Orthodox church.

. Sunday, October 17, 1948 .

Mrs. Wanda Chause Clements . . . Hunting mishap takes her life.

Wanda C. Clements

Mrs. Clements

Funeral services for Mrs. Wanda Chause Clements, 23, of 1823 South Main St., who died Saturday, will be conducted Wednesday at 2 p.m. in the Greek Orthodox Holy Trinity Church, Second West and Third South Streets. Friends may call at 36 East Seventh South St., Tuesday and at 3774 Ninth East Wednesday from 10 a.m. until time of funeral Burial will be in Mt. Olivet Cemetery.

From the Front Page of the Salt Lake Tribune, October 17, 1948

After I put the boxes away, Aunt Wanda was on my mind for days. Then, about a week later, I received a call from my cousin Steve, Anne's youngest son. I hadn't seen or heard from him in years, so I was a little surprised. Steve always had a big smile on his face, but he wasn't always happy. He was Anne's youngest child and caretaker until the day she died. His oldest brother, Rick, who had survived the Vietnam War, had recently died of lung cancer at 65.

"Hi, Margie. It's your cousin. It's Steve," he said.

"Hello, Steve! I've been thinking about you lately. I'm sorry I wasn't able to make it to Utah for Rick's funeral. How are you?"

"I'm okay. It's difficult with both my mom and brother gone. There is a big space in my life right now. I've been spending a lot of time visiting the cemetery. In fact, that's why I'm calling. Every time I go to the cemetery, I visit all the relatives. Grandma, Grandpa, and Aunt Wanda are in a different area, across from the sisters and my brother Rick. Uncle Jim is all by himself. It's so sad to see Wanda's tombstone. The picture of her is completely destroyed."

"Yes, I remember that. In fact, I remember the picture of Wanda on her tombstone before it was vandalized." It was a beautiful image.

"Well, I want to restore it. I've done some research and I need a photograph of her to replace the one that's been destroyed. Do you happen to have a photograph of Aunt Wanda?"

I was silent for a minute. Was it just a simple twist of fate that my cousin was calling me just a few days after I had opened up that box of my mother's treasures? Pandora's Box?

Not only did I have a photo of Wanda, it was the same photo as the one on her tombstone. The one that was smashed.

Bless my mother and her hoarding skills.

"Steve, you won't believe this. I was going through some of Mom's boxes a while ago and I saw that photo of Aunt Wanda—the same one that's on her tombstone! I remember it from when I was a child. It's an oval-shaped, professional photograph. What a coincidence! I love your idea to restore her tombstone. You are amazing! "

Was it truly just a coincidence?

"Would you be willing to send it to me so I can restore her tombstone?" he asked.

"Of course, I'll send you the photo. You will probably need the original photograph, so I'll make a copy before I send it."

"Oh, I almost forgot. I have one more question...Do you know why Chaus is spelled with an **e** on the end [Chause] on some of the gravestones but without the **e** [Chaus] on others?" he asked.

"I am not sure," I said, "I've seen it spelled both ways over the years—most recently the family spelled it without the e on the end."

"That's strange. Thank you so much, Margie."

"You are welcome, Steve. I'm glad I happened to see that photo in Mom's stuff a few days ago. Keep in touch and let me know how it goes."

"I will let you know for sure," he said.

I sent the photo, along with a check for $50 to help him with expenses. A few days later, I received an email.

> Wow
> i got your letter today, and it is special to me.
> i am going to move forward with wanda's pic.
> your check is probably going to be torn up. by me.
> thanks for the thought
> i am dealing with ricks will.
> he has some assets. and i am the executor.
> so i have several people to deal with,
> and 2 properties to transfer to his kids.
> and a couple of accounts with assets to distribute.
> just a look into my life.
> talk to you soon.

i like the e mail.

its cheaper than a phone call.

thanks to you!

A few weeks later...I received another email from Steve. No message. Just two photos of Wanda's tombstone—before and after the restoration. In yet another twist of fate, the **before** photo of Wanda's tombstone, taken in late fall, was surrounded by brown grass and bare trees. The **after** photo, taken in the spring, was surrounded by green grass and leafy trees. Wanda's tombstone had sprung back to life.

Wanda's Tombstone: Before and After Steve's Restoration Project

I responded immediately.

You know, Steve, I think our relatives are looking down at this and feeling very grateful for you. I hope to be in Utah next year for Memorial Day, so I will get to see it in person...How are you doing?

He responded the very next day...

I am doing very well. How About you?

By then, I had moved back to Minneapolis.

I'm happy to be back in Minnesota. Let's keep in touch. I can't
wait to see Wanda's tombstone when I come to Utah.

After our email exchange, I got busy with my work and didn't spend
a lot of time thinking about my young cousin.

A year later, I was planning a trip to Utah over Memorial Day
Weekend. I had organized an event with my sisters and cousins to honor
Steve for his restoration of Wanda's tombstone at Mt. Olivet Cemetery.
We were going to meet at the cemetery at noon on Memorial Day.
Afterwards, we would have lunch at The Other Place, a Greek family
restaurant in Salt Lake City. It was a family tradition to gather together
after a trip to the cemetery on Memorial Day and I was looking forward
to a celebratory reunion with my mother's family in honor of Steve and
Aunt Wanda.

A couple of days before my flight, I got a call from Steve's niece,
Vanessa. Her voice was muffled and she spoke slowly.

"Margie," she said. "...Steve is gone."

"What? I'm getting ready for my trip to Utah right now. Where did
he go? We are planning to honor him on Monday at the cemetery. "

"Margie...this is so hard for me," Vanessa said. "I got a call from
Steve's manager this morning. He was worried because Steve didn't
come to work this morning. I had no idea where he might be. I offered
to check it out and get back to him. As soon as I hung up the phone, I
drove to Steve's house. I unlocked the door and walked in. Everything
seemed normal. I called out for Steve. No answer. Then I noticed a note

on the kitchen table. It was a suicide note. He told me to drive to the West Desert and find his car. By then, I was shaking. My whole body was in shock. I called the police and they arrived within minutes. They said I should go with them to find Steve. I was praying we'd find him alive. Well, his car was right where he said it would be, but he wasn't inside. I stayed in the police car while they walked into the desert."

Vanessa stopped for a minute to catch her breath.

"Margie....he shot himself...in the head ... with a 22-caliber pistol."

"Oh my God!" I screamed.

This news felt like a shot in the heart. Why did I not see it coming?

As it turns out, no one saw it coming. On the Wednesday before Memorial Day, Steve took the day off. He visited his brother George, who lived in a group home. Steve spent much of the day chatting with him. According to Vanessa, his final words to his brother were, "Goodbye, George. I love you." The next day, he drove into a remote area of the West Desert, parked his car on the side of the road, and hiked to a dry, quiet area where he ceremoniously shot himself in the head.

Unaware of the deep, dark secret my cousin had been keeping, I can see it now more clearly as I re-read his brief email messages to me—all typed in lowercase.

The theme song from the movie, M.A.S.H., "Suicide is Painless" plays in my mind.

Did he feel any pain after he pulled the trigger?

Steven Brent Swartz was born on August 11, 1959. He is buried at Mount Olivet Cemetery, along with the other Chaus relatives, except Uncle George who is buried near his wife's family—eternally estranged from the rest of the family. As it turned out, Steve knew our whole family would be in Utah on Memorial Day, so he planned his own reunion—his funeral.

In his will, he had requested a Greek Orthodox funeral. However, according to church doctrine, "Thou shalt not kill" includes suicide because "all life is a gift from God." Sadly, Steve was unaware of that doctrine when he requested a church funeral. Although Vanessa tried to convince the priest to honor his wish, the best he could do was offer a simple Memorial Service at the mortuary and a graveside prayer at the cemetery.

As I stood there at Mt. Olivet, I thought about the fact that just a few weeks ago, I was looking forward to a celebration of Steve's connection with Wanda, a sign that the trauma of our family's past had finally come to a place of healing. Instead, there I was, mourning yet another untimely death in the family. My generation had now experienced the trauma of a violent death directly, not indirectly through our parents' generation.

~

Keeping steadfast love for thousands, forgiving iniquity and
transgression and sin, but who will by no means clear the
guilty, visiting the iniquity of the fathers on the children and
the children's children, to the third and the fourth generation.

—EXODUS 34:7

I DID NOT know William Clements, Wanda's husband. I know he shot
Wanda in the heart during the Deer Hunting Mishap, a fact that was
documented in the Salt Lake Tribune on October 17, 1948. I also know
"he was already married to another woman" when he married my aunt
on November 7, 1947. So, when I began writing these stories, I searched
the internet to learn more about this man who was my uncle by marriage for almost a year.

During my internet research, I discovered an interview with his
son, Clark, for a local public television series called "Utah Vietnam War
Stories." Finding that interview was like discovering a buried treasure.

Clark Tyler Clements was born the same year my grandmother died
of a broken heart. He is the second son of William and Donna Clements
and was a student at South High School, my alma mater. Although he
is three years younger than I am, surely our paths crossed while we were
growing up.

Reading the interview gave me a glimpse of William Clements' other family. In 1968, Clark's best friend, Brent, convinced him to join the Marines. The Vietnam war had begun and young men were being drafted. The two of them chose to enlist instead.

Clark was an unlikely candidate for the Marine Corps with his long hair, but he followed his friend's advice. During the interview, he described how his friend convinced him to join the Marine Corps. They went through a rigorous training program with the Marines and were sent to the front lines together. Clark describes the sounds, smells, and sights in the aftermath of that mission in Vietnam.

At some point, Clark lost contact with Brent. Although he was on the front lines, Brent was safely following somewhere behind him. One day, Clark tried to communicate with his friend. He wrote to him using an in-country postcard, pleading with him not to stay back, away from the front lines.

In the fog of war, no news is not necessarily good news. The postcard he sent to Brent was returned with no response. Still, he held out hope that they would be reunited. Then, the following spring, Clark received a letter from his cousin in Utah. His cousin broke the news that Brent was dead.

Clark survived the Vietnam War. However, he paid a big price. When he came home, he was unable to share the anger and pain he experienced during the war, even with those closest to him. A victim of PTSD, he also had a deep fear of intimacy. He described how, whenever he started to get close, he would see the specter of death. Ultimately, he and his first wife divorced..

Had the Deer Hunting Mishap touched his life as well?

After reading his story over and over, I decided to write to him. I sent him a copy of the newspaper clippings I had found in my mother's treasures.

April 30, 2015

Dear Clark,

I know letter writing is not very common these days, but I think this may be the best way to make contact with you. And I hope we will, someday, have an opportunity to meet in person.

In the past couple of years, I've been doing some family research and I realized that we have a connection to each other. I grew up in Salt Lake City and moved to Minneapolis 25 years ago with my daughter. My son was just starting college and I had been a single mom for 10 years. I graduated from South High School in 1965, so I'm old enough to take a chance and reach out to you. So, here goes...

I grew up knowing about my Aunt Wanda's short life, but in the process of researching my family's history, I found even more information, which led me to you.

It is old news, but powerful, and I was moved to learn more when I found the enclosed obituary in my mother's memorabilia. Your father and my aunt had been married for a year and a half when the deer hunting mishap occurred. If this is the first you have heard about the incident, it will be "new" news to you. In any case, this is how we are connected.

My mom always said that my grandmother died of a "broken heart." And, in doing the research, I realized that she died a year after the mishap. She was in her early fifties. The women in my mother's generation had relationship problems throughout their lives and, a generation later, divorce is still pretty common in our family. To add to the sadness, my cousin, who recently refurbished Aunt Wanda's tombstone, committed suicide shortly afterward. He was just 53 years old.

During my research, I found a KUED interview with you. Your story touched my heart and I began to wonder whether this mishap also had an impact on your life and your family's lives. I'd very much like to meet you someday--if you are willing. I have included my contact information just in case.

May all love surround you and yours.

I signed the printed letter and included my address and phone number. Then, I sent it off to the address I found online, wondering whether or not I would hear back from him.

A few months later, I got a phone call. I glanced at the caller ID. It was a call from Utah. I didn't recognize the phone number, just the area code.

"Hello."

"Hello. Is this Margie?"

"Yes, it is."

"This is Clark Clements."

(How did he know my family called me Margie?)

"Oh, hello, Clark," I said as I settled into my favorite chair.

"I got your letter in the mail and thought I'd give you a call. My nephew, Tyler, was here earlier today and we were talking about Wanda. He's my brother's son and he's named after me. My middle name is Tyler," he said.

Then, he jumped right to the purpose of his call.

"I know the story about your aunt. She would have been my step-mom. My mother told me the whole story when I was 13 years old—the same story that was in the newspaper clipping you sent."

At that moment, I felt like I had just opened up Pandora's box.

"It was an accident," he said, emphatically, explaining that his father had taught him how to handle a gun and sharing his own experience with the fog of war in Vietnam.

"My parents were separated when Dad married your aunt," he said.

"Really? So, they were not living together?"

"No...But...oh my," he said. "I just realized something. That means my dad was a bigamist."

Pause.

So, it's true. William was still married to his first wife when he married Wanda in 1947.

"I'm glad it wasn't a surprise," I said. "I was afraid it may have been a shock."

"Well, as it turns out, my father deserted us twice. He came back after Wanda died and, after I was born. Then, he left again."

"Tell me about your mom," I said.

"My mother was like a Buddhist. She wouldn't kill an ant. Actually, she was married three times. One of her husbands was into music and he was a big influence on me when I was 18. Anyway, I almost married a Greek girl. She was older than me and she was Brent's girlfriend in high school. Her name was Diana. We lived together after my divorce. At one point, I thought about asking her to marry me. She was my best friend ever and, she was Greek."

"We probably went to the same church," I said.

"Well, I knew my dad had married this beautiful Greek girl and I believe somehow, the specter of Wanda's death came between us. I don't know. Maybe I was afraid something would happen to her if we got married. And then, I couldn't believe it. She was killed in a train wreck."

"A train wreck?"

"Yeah. Diana married another guy and they were separated at the time. She had already filed for a divorce. Then, one night, she was driving home on the west side of town and she was hit by a train. Diana would never have tried to cross the tracks if a train was coming," he said.

"It wasn't an accident. I just know it wasn't an accident."

"In fact," he went on, "when I saw Diana's mother at the funeral, she said to me, 'Clark, if you'd have married her, this never would have happened.'"

"I'm so sorry, Clark," I said.

His words reverberated in my mind. *"It wasn't an accident!"* My thoughts scattered like ashes in the wind. I thought about my family the night they learned about Wanda's death. I thought about Clark the night he learned about Diana's death. I thought about Clark's brother, William Jr. (What happened to him anyway?)

Clark was born two years after Wanda died. His brother Bill, named after his father, was born in 1943. He was 4 years old when William and Wanda were married. I wanted to know more.

"How about your brother?" I asked.

"My brother Bill was a wild man and a musician," Clark said. "He taught me how to play the guitar. When my parents divorced, he went to live with my dad and I stayed with my mom. Dad was in a fragile state, so when he met Darlene, who was a really strong woman, he married her. She took good care of him. But she and my brother didn't get along."

I listened carefully, wanting to know more, even though that small detail about his brother and Darlene was not a big surprise. I had read his father's obituary and William Jr. was not even mentioned. I had also read Clark's mother's obituary. Donna died at 47 in 1975. Her obituary states the cause of death as "pending a report from the state medical examiner" and lists William Phillip Jr. and Clark Tyler Clements as two of her surviving sons.

Clark did not want to talk about his brother. He said he had recently spent time with him in hospice before he died.

"My brother was a bad boy."

He stopped short of telling me more. At some point, he mentioned the biblical phrase, "the sins of the father," and told me I should be afraid of men. I didn't press him for more information.

I did some more research after our conversation.

William Phillip Clements Jr. **was** a bad boy. In 1966, he was charged with assault with intent to commit rape. He was 23 years old—the same age as my aunt when she was shot in the heart by his father.

On September 1, 1971, William Jr.'s wife was granted a divorce and custody of their child. He was charged with "cruel treatment."

Did the sins of his father pass, epigenetically, on to his namesake? I can only wonder at this point.

∼

A FEW MONTHS later, Clark called again. It was fall in Minnesota. October 2015. The maple leaves on the tree in my front yard were changing from green to yellow and from yellow to tangerine in a palette of all three colors. Deer hunting season had begun and political ads were in full swing, even though the 45th presidential election was a year away. I'd just finished watching PBS NewsHour and I was thinking about going to bed early to read. I locked the doors, turned off the TV and started switching off the lights.

"Night night, Zuzu," I said gently to my 3-year old Tibetan Terrier. Zuzu is named after George Bailey's little girl in the Christmas movie, "It's a Wonderful Life." She understands simple phrases like, "Walk," "Go," "Come," "Treat," "Ouch," "Bye-Bye," "I'll be back," and "Night, Night."

My iPhone rang and I glanced at the caller ID. It was Clark. I pressed the green button and answered with hesitation, hoping it wasn't bad news.

"Hello."

"Hi, Margie. It's Clark. Is this a good time to talk?"

"Yes... Of course." I was surprised to hear from him again.

"How are you?" I asked as I sat down at the dining table. Zuzu settled in under the table, at my feet.

"I'm doing well. I just wanted to let you know I went to Mt. Olivet to visit Wanda. In fact, I went there twice. First, I went with my two cousins on my dad's side of the family—Dale Myerberg and Dave Clements. The next day, I went back alone," he said. "Have you heard of Dale Myerberg? He's a world-renowned national Yoyo master!"

No," I said..."I'll have to google him."

It's true! Dale is a Yoyo master.

"Anyway, we all got together for lunch and then we went to the cemetery. We talked about my dad and Aunt Wanda. They remember her well."

"Thank you so much, Clark. That is so sweet of you to visit my aunt at the cemetery."

"You know, when we saw Wanda's beautiful picture on her headstone, it brought back a lot of memories for my cousins. Dave said he and his dad used to visit my father and Wanda at their apartment near State Street and 8th South," said Clark.

Wow! I was getting a glimpse into Wanda's life before she died.

"He said my dad was devastated after Wanda died. He just moped around and was pretty much useless. According to Dave, he disappeared for three years after I was born."

I remembered our first conversation when Clark said his father had "deserted the family twice."

"Oh, by the way," he said, "I noticed that Wanda's last name on her headstone is not Clements. It's Chause. Her maiden name. And, what does the W stand for?"

"The W?" I asked, confused.

"Yes. It's the middle initial on her tombstone."

"Hmm... I have no idea," I said, trying to remember the inscription on her tombstone.

Why had I had never noticed the W on Wanda's tombstone? Wanda's maiden name was inscribed on her tombstone, even though her married name was Clements. That makes sense. Her husband shot her in the heart. But what does that W stand for? She didn't have a middle name.

Traditionally, Greek girls were not given a middle name. Once they married, their maiden name became their middle name. Did the W stand for Wife? She was a Daughter and a Wife. I also noticed another strange detail. Wanda died on October 16, 1948, but the date of her death on her tombstone is November 16, 1948:

DAUGHTER

WANDA W. CHAUSE

DEC 5, 1924

NOV 16, 1948 [sic]

"Anyway, after I got home, I remembered something I can't get out of my head," said Clark. "There was a baby deer resting right next to Wanda's grave. The deer was not afraid at all. She looked right at me. And her eyes were so big and brown. They reminded me of Wanda's eyes."

Mount Olivet is a favorite hangout for deer, but chills ran down my back when Clark said he saw a baby deer next to Wanda's tombstone looking up at him.

"The collective unconscious is all around us," he said. "We just need to open our eyes and see it. By the way, I also found Diana at Mount Olivet. You know, I think the last name on her headstone should be her maiden name. She was almost divorced. She should be remembered by her maiden name—just like Wanda."

"I know what you mean," I said. "I'm sure my grandparents wanted to remember Wanda as their daughter."

"...Anyway," Clark continued, "I want to thank you for bringing me back together with my dad's side of the family. I grew up with my mother, so I didn't spend much time with my dad's family," he said. "As it turns out, death creates a space in life. Now that my brother is gone, I'm inspired to plan a memorial for him. Although I was with him when he died, we never had a service for him. He's gone and he deserves one."

"Yes," I said, "Your brother deserves a memorial service. Thank you for sharing this with me."

"You are welcome, and thank you. Good night, Margie."

As I pressed the end call button on my phone, I was reminded of Clark's reference to "the sins of the father" during our last phone conversation. Lucky for him, he was raised by a mother with Buddhist leanings. "She wouldn't kill an ant."

> Don't hold the iniquities of our forefathers against us. Let your tender mercies speedily meet us, for we are in desperate need.
>
> —PSALM 79:8

~

GROWING UP WITH a mother who was often unable to express herself openly and honestly was difficult for me. And, I believe her deep-seated anger worked its way into my life. My own anger was sometimes so deep it took me years to realize what was happening.

Jami, Debbie, Mary, Kathy, and Me, Two Harbors, MN 2004

Like my mother and her sisters, my sisters and I have fun times and spirited conversation together, punctuated with bouts of yelling and talking about each other instead of talking with each other.

"You sound just like mom!"

"She has no idea how I feel!"

"I'm not depressed. I'm just sad!"

"That's crazy!"

Sometimes it takes a stranger to make us aware of our strong matriarchal legacy. One weekend, we were all together shopping for groceries during one of our periodic sister getaways when another shopper made an observation out loud.

"You girls remind me of a Chinese fire drill," he said.

We each had our own idea about what to buy for dinner as we darted in different directions. Sisterhood. We are all strong, independent women. It runs in the family.

In 1981, I left my teaching job to join the corporate world and asked my sister Kathy to help me invest my small retirement fund. She was a financial planner at the time and I trusted her with my savings.

I had pretty much forgotten about it until I changed jobs again, ten years later when I decided to consolidate my retirement funds and transfer my Utah account into my new retirement savings account. I didn't even think to call Kathy for help because she had moved to California with a different company and she was no longer managing that small retirement savings account.

I assumed it would be a simple transfer from one retirement account to another, so I contacted the bank in Utah and requested a transfer to my new retirement account in Minnesota. To my surprise, I was charged a $2,000 fee to transfer the funds from one retirement account to another. To make matters worse, the amount of my investment had not grown at all in ten years! It was still $15,000. I was surprised and angry. Did I call my sister and ask her why? Of course not. Instead, I tucked my anger away in a box. Pandora's Box?

There it stayed. Or so I thought. It is never that simple. Like my grandfather's unspoken anger at his oldest son who sold the family property gifted to him and my mother's pent up anger at her sister over my brother's missing stamp collection, I carried my own unspoken anger around with me throughout most of my adult life. It came between Kathy and me every time we were together, and even when we were not together. Emails, side conversations with my other sisters, and even face-to-face blowups just served to deepen my unresolved anger.

"Stop interrupting me!" I yelled at my sister as we strolled through the quiet grounds at the Red Truck Winery in Sonoma California. Then, I went on, berating and belittling my sister in front of my sister-in-law and anyone else nearby who was there to enjoy the beauty of the valley. That is just one outburst I recall clearly. It took me 35 years to realize what was brewing behind my many angry, judgmental reactions, usually around money.

When I retired and looked more carefully at my retirement savings, I had time to explore my own behavior. As I reviewed my retirement savings to analyze the funds in my savings, Pandora's box opened up. That small retirement fund I had moved from Utah to Minnesota was the source of all my angry outbursts toward Kathy. I picked up the phone and called my sister to apologize.

"Kathy, I think I figured out what has been getting in the way of my relationship with you for all these years," I said. "Do you remember when you helped me to open a $15,000 retirement savings account when you worked as a financial planner in Utah?

"I'm afraid I don't," she said.

My usual response would have been to chide her for not remembering. Not this time.

"Well, I decided to transfer it into another retirement account after I moved to Minnesota so I could consolidate my funds," I said. "As it turned out, I was charged a $2,000 fee and my initial investment had not grown at all."

"Oh my, Margie...Why didn't you call me back then? I don't remember it at all," said my sister.

"I don't know what I was thinking," I said. "I just assumed you weren't managing it anymore so you wouldn't be able to help me."

"Let me think," she said. "Maybe I invested your savings in an annuity to pay regular dividends <u>after</u> you retired. That would explain the early withdrawal fee as well as the amount of money available."

I had no idea there would be a penalty since it was a retirement account. Like many women of my generation, I was financially illiterate. The word annuity makes sense now, but back then, I didn't understand the fine print. I just handed it over to my sister to do what she thought was best for me.

"Really? I had no idea it was an annuity. I do wish I'd have called you back then. It's all over now. And I want to apologize for my behavior over the years. Please forgive me."

"Margie, I sure wish you'd have called me back then when I could have helped you. I'm so sorry."

"Me too. I am deeply sorry I allowed this to interfere with our relationship."

Up until that moment in time, I was unaware of how well I had mastered the passive aggressive techniques I denounced in others—silent treatment, shunning, ignoring, and stonewalling. Despite my deep respect for direct and clear communication, I had unconsciously inherited my grandfather's stubbornness and my mother's anger.

Was my own anger a reincarnation of the anger expressed by my grandfather? My uncle? My mother? Did I "inherit" my reactions from previous generations, epigenetically?

I am so grateful that I was able to let go of the wall I had erected between my sister and me (a wall as high as the Great Wall of China, or the Berlin Wall, or Donald Trump's Border Wall). Once I became aware of my own behavior, I breathed a huge sigh of relief as the wall between us came tumbling down. Regardless of their origin, I deeply regret every unexamined reaction to my sister.

The road to redemption can be a long, winding road. For me, I first had to recognize my own unspoken anger. Then, I had to accept responsibility for my actions and ask my sister to forgive me. Finally, I had to forgive myself, a difficult but necessary step along the way.

Ultimately, I also had to forgive my mother.

Ever the memory keeper, after Mom passed away, I had an opportunity to choose one of her rings as a keepsake. When I glanced at each of the rings displayed carefully in my sister's guest room, there was no hesitation. I knew immediately which ring I would choose —Grandma's wedding ring. Though it is the least valuable ring (financially), it is the most valuable to me in terms of our family's history. I chose the ring my mother wore every day at the end of her life. I wear that ring every day, a reminder of the healing power of acceptance and forgiveness after generations of grief and trauma.

Mom greeting her nephew, Michael Chaus in Salt Lake City, August, 2008

The next generation of the Chaus family is coming together. What a gift it is to celebrate with our cousins after all these years. We are on Facebook and we keep in touch with each other from time to time over the phone. The past no longer guides the present.

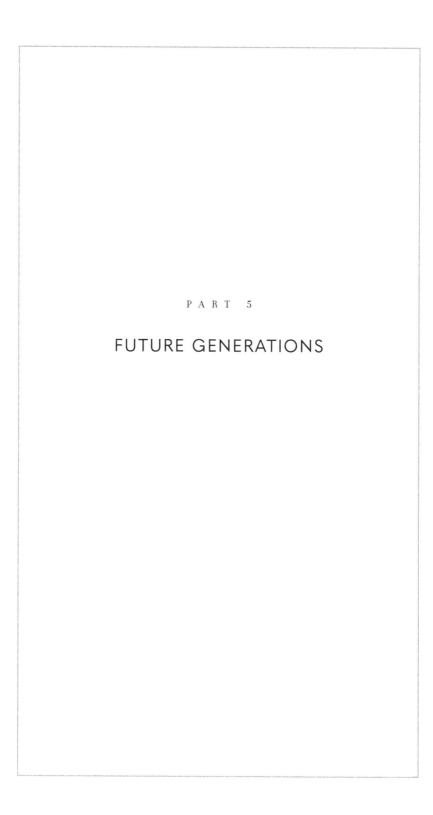

PART 5

FUTURE GENERATIONS

FORGIVENESS

~

As I watch over our family, it's like I'm watching a movie. Each generation knows my pain. There was no autopsy, but Mama knew I was carrying a baby. She just knew things. Now she is happy to be with me. We watch over all the children, grandchildren, and great grandchildren. Sometimes they visit me at Mt. Olivet Cemetery where the deer roam freely.

—WANDA

FOR THREE GENERATIONS, our family unconsciously carried around various stages of grief. My grandmother burned incense, begging God to forgive her. She walked five miles each way to visit her daughter at Mount Olivet cemetery and buried her grief in a trunk, along with the red sweater Wanda was wearing the night she died. She tried to focus on her grandchildren, but her eyes, windows to her soul, were sad.

Unable to honor Wanda's memory by celebrating her life, my grandmother fell deeper into depression as she continued to mourn her death. Two years after Wanda died, my grandmother's heart strings snapped. She died of a *broken heart*, passing her grief on to the next generation.

After Grandma died, my grandfather leased the family farm to friends and wandered aimlessly from Aunt Alice's home to Aunt Anne's home in a perpetual state of sadness. He longed for his wife, his daughter, and his farm as he went through the motions of living. The heavy weight of his loss often erupted in anger as he lashed out at his own children. His ultimate act of revenge was to remove his oldest son from his will, passing his grief down to the entire family as his anger spilled over into his children's relationships with each other.

Uncle George was a victim of my grandfather's grief. He just happened to be the oldest son, the one sibling who was removed from Grandpa's will because he chose not to take over the family farm—even though he worked on the farm until he left for the Army in 1945.

In a sense, we're all victims of Grandpa's grief, a grief that inspired the big family schism and separated our families for years. Our generation is responding to that trauma by bringing the family back together—finally.

Aunt Anne, the oldest Chaus daughter, who had plenty of her own trauma, lived much of her life in denial. She danced her way through life, falling from time to time, yet always bouncing back onto the dance floor. She was a survivor. Her three sons were not so lucky. They never knew their biological fathers and they each struggled in their own way. Their responses to the trauma included chronic pain, alcoholism, schizophrenia, depression, and suicide.

Aunt Alice was practical and headstrong. She buried her grief in secrets and lies. A secret marriage. A sister's secret pregnancy. A secret affair. A secret baby. Alice's little altar of icons and candles on her nightstand was a symbol of her prayers for forgiveness, her bargain with God. When the truth behind her own secret is finally revealed, the trauma will pass on to the next generation.

My mother, Afton, was full of contradiction. She married my father and was a loyal wife during their marriage, even though she always wondered whether she should have married another man. She was fiercely judgmental toward Aunt Anne until the day she died. She alternated between being a loving, caring mother and a paranoid, distrustful woman convinced that strangers were out to get her. My mother's grief was often expressed as a desire to control herself and those around her.

James ("Jimmy") Chaus, the youngest child, spent his entire adult life in the psychiatric ward at the Veteran's Hospital in Salt Lake City, a victim of Post-Traumatic Stress Syndrome before there was a name for it. He returned from the war in 1946, two years before the Deer Hunting Mishap. Although he never married or had any children, his presence at family events was a constant reminder of gun violence for me. I knew he had accidentally shot one of his own.

We each respond to trauma in our own way. I react to war, mass shootings, homicides, suicides, and suddenly, a global coronavirus epidemic with a sense of fear and anxiety reminiscent of the trauma my mother's generation experienced.

Accidents happen, but bad accidents and gun violence have reverberated in our family for generations. Every time I see a bleeding deer on the road or in the bed of a truck, I go back to the Deer Hunting Mishap, consciously or unconsciously. It's as though I saw it happen. Paradoxically, my own reaction to my mother's paranoia was to trust others indiscriminately. I resisted her superstition and mistrust by becoming too trusting. I have also been known to echo her desire for being in control, but I am learning to let go, slowly.

"Let it be...let it be...let it be."

EPILOGUE

~

WANDA HAS BEEN gone for more than 70 years. She lies between my grandparents, William and Katina, the only member of my mother's family with a tall, upright tombstone.

I am the oldest girl in my family. I was just 9 months old when Wanda married William Clements and 19 months old when he shot her in the heart. For as long as I can remember, Wanda has been my Guardian Angel. She instilled in me a deep reverence for life and I believe she is guiding me to help her heal the pain of the past and bring peace to future generations.

On Memorial Day 2017, I was in Salt Lake City, Utah. Liz and Michael took me to Mt. Olivet Cemetery to visit Wanda's grave site. As we made our way, weaving through a sea of graves, flowers, and flags toward my Aunt Wanda's tombstone, Liz gently rearranged any potted plants that had tipped over in the wind. She was carrying Sophie Anne inside her.

I am thinking about my grandmother and my mother, both of whom raised six children, my two beautiful children, and my three brilliant grandchildren. I carry them with me wherever I go.

Now that the stories are told, it's time to forgive ourselves, our ancestors, and each other. It's time to shower the next generation with love and gratitude for those who went before us.

"I am my mother, but I'm not.

I am my grandmother, but I'm not.

I am my great-grandmother, but I am not."

—TERRY TEMPEST WILLIAMS, *WHEN WOMEN WERE BIRDS:*

FIFTY-FOUR VARIATIONS ON VOICE